Productivity Economics

Making Capitalism Work Again

By Ronald Hart

Productivity Economics

ISBN-13: 978-1530177455

ISBN-10: 1530177456

Front cover images under license from Thinkstock by Getty Images

CS 0319d

Dedication

To my parents who sacrificed so that their children could get a good education and professional careers.

This was the stuff of family dinner conversations when I was young.

Thanks to my wife and my brothers for their help and support with this book.

Table of Contents

List of Figures

1. A World of Economic Problems

The Western World is experiencing many economic problems. There are some very large issues in our society that are going to define how the future unfolds. Symptoms of a system that is not working include stagnant economies, deflation, worldwide unemployment, falling standards of living for most of the Ninety-Nine Percent, social unrest in many parts of the world, the Occupy Wall Street movement, the Europe Crisis, the Greek Crisis, terrorism, the inability of the bottom half of the social economic pyramid to better themselves, government deficit and debt problems, and excessive private debt.

For many in the United States, this is the first time that they have experienced a declining standard of living. This is the first time that a majority believe that the next generation will have a lower standard of living than their parents.

People are discontented. They no longer believe that the system is working for them, or that it will work for them in the future.

Many believe that the cause of the problem is the increasing disparity between the wealth of the One Percent and the other Ninety-Nine Percent. More and more people believe that the solution is to increase taxes on the rich and to redistribute the proceeds to the middle class and lower income citizens.

Falling standards of living and the increasing disparity between the wealth of the One Percent and The Ninety-Nine Percent are a result of world social economic changes that have been mismanaged. Wealth disparity is a symptom of the problem, not the cause. Wealth redistribution will only make things worse in the long term.

This book provides new insights into the root causes of the problems and proposes changes that will restore the economy to a path of growing prosperity and improving standards of living for all workers.

2. The Big Picture

We are in an "era of abundance." Everything is abundant: energy, materials, minerals, textiles, transportation, food, labor, computing power, manufactured goods, and especially money. Supply exceeds demand in virtually every segment of the economy, except perhaps water. Prices are stagnant or are being driven downwards. Companies do not have pricing power. Corporate revenues are stagnant, particularly for US domestic companies.

Regulators do not have an effective way to stimulate the economy when a recession pushes the economy into low inflation or deflation. Japan has suffered from this for decades and has tried all the conventional solutions, to no avail. Now much of Europe and the Americas is in a similar position and teeters on the edge of deflation.

The risk of deflation is very real. Deflation is an economic disaster for the working person and for governments. It leads to overwhelming debt and a falling standard of living for everyone except the rich. If persistent deflation takes hold it is likely that a depression will follow.

Interest rates are near zero or even negative in most of the G8 countries, and some central banks are printing money at a breakneck pace.

Low-income and middle-class wages are stagnant or falling in most Western countries. The middle class is being diminished.

There is high unemployment among youth, minorities, and unskilled workers.

Productivity Economics

Government debt is becoming unsustainable in many countries.

Governments are implementing austerity programs around the world.

Savings rates are low.

Many pension plans are underfunded and at risk of long-term default.

Life insurance plans are becoming non-viable.[1, 2]

Social problems and social violence are increasing.

These problems are likely to be made worse by the so called "Fourth Industrial Revolution," in which Artificial Intelligence, robotics, and 3D printing displace more and more workers. This was one of the major themes at the 2015 World Economic Forum meeting in Davos, Switzerland.[3]

None of the politicians in the 2016 USA presidential contest or the G20 governments have proposed a solution that has a credible chance of leading to a solution of the fundamental problems.

3. The Real Issue

The real issue isn't the increasing wealth and income gap between the rich and the rest. The real issue is that the standard of living is falling for most of the US population.

Figure 3-1 Chart of Household Income Trend by Income Quintile

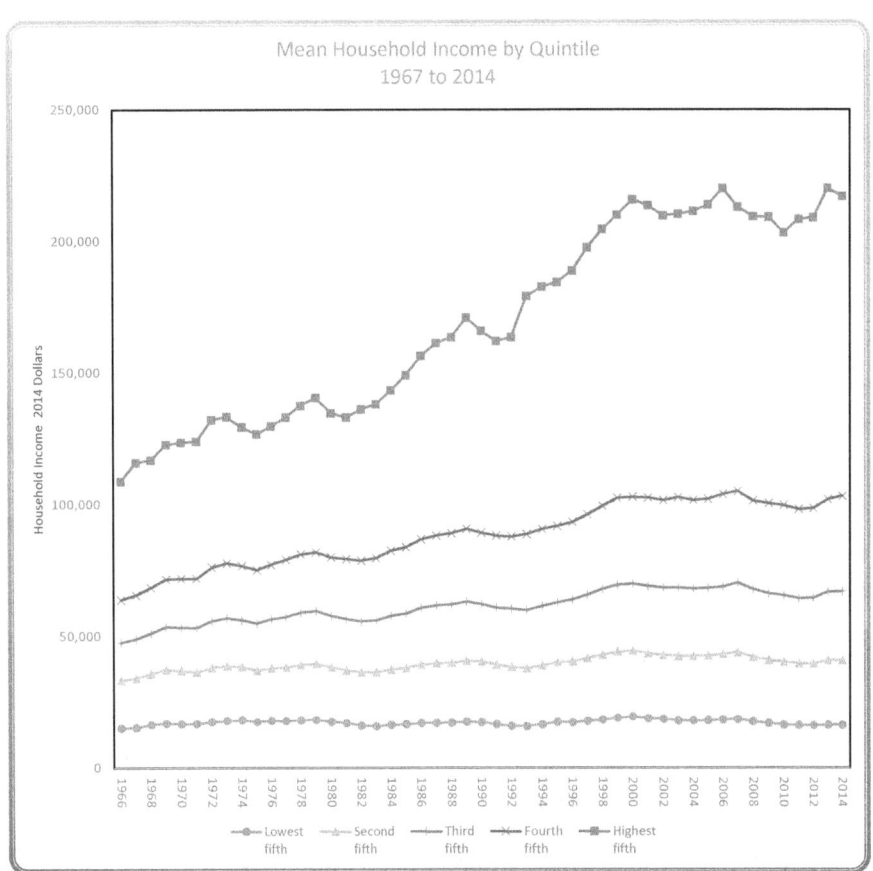

Source: US Census Bureau; Table F1

Figure 3.1 shows that since 2000 nearly everyone's incomes have been decreasing. Low incomes have not increased since 1970 and they have been decreasing since 2000. It is not just unskilled workers who are being left behind; incomes of the entire middle class are also falling. Low and middle income workers have good reason to be angry. The economy is not working for them.

Figure 3-2 Chart of Median Earnings by Education

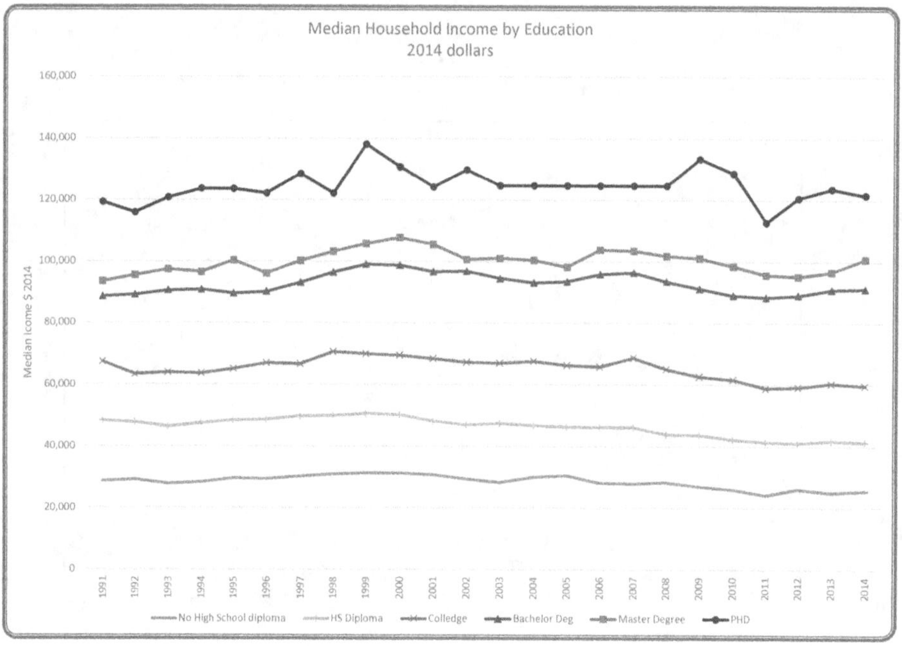

Source: US Census Bureau: Table H13

Figure 3.2 shows that education or qualifications are not sufficient to ensure future prosperity. Both the median income and the income for high school grads have been flat since 1990. Incomes for people with bachelor's and master's degrees have been falling since 1999. The only people who continue to prosper are the rich, who earn their income from capital investments rather than wages.

Making Capitalism Work Again

Median means the middle data point. Median income is the income point where exactly 50 percent of workers earn more and 50 percent earn less. This book uses "median income" figures rather than average income because average income values are highly distorted by the extremely high incomes of the One Percent.

There are several different views about how the problem of falling incomes and the divergence of income and wealth between the rich and wage earners should be solved.

One school of thought is that nothing should be done. The market will self-correct and everything will be fine. As this book explains, globalization and automation make this highly unlikely.

Another school of thought is that if the tax system is fixed and rationalized and taxes are lowered, the problem will be solved. Tax changes are necessary, but as shown, this is not nearly sufficient to solve the problem.

A third school of thought is that there should be ***income redistribution*** where the taxes on the rich are increased and the proceeds used to support better education, health care, and to supplement incomes for the poor, or even implement a *"basic income."* This may work, at least in the short term, but it is not the best solution and it has serious consequences for democracy and capitalism.

The best solution is *"**income participation**,"* as proposed in this book. *Income participation* is not new. It was one of the primary drivers of the Golden Age of Capitalism between 1945 and 1970, when the economy boomed and incomes and standards of living grew rapidly for all income groups.

The resolution of the problems of falling incomes and the increasing wealth gap has fundamental social, economic, and political implications that are discussed in this book.

All people want is enough income to meet their needs for food, shelter and clothing, security, some entertainment, meaning in their life, and a sense of independence and freedom. Perhaps most importantly, they want to believe that the future will be better for them and their children.

Numerous studies illustrate that once these conditions are met, subject to being safe, socially connected and healthy, people are happy. The issue isn't that the One Percent have too much. It is that the fundamental needs are not being met for over half of the US population, and many believe that they won't be met in their lifetime.

The single most important metric for a functioning society is that the standard of living for low-income and middle-income people meaningfully increase over time. Standard of living includes income, wealth, health, personal safety and education.

If people believe that the future doesn't have much of a future, then society destabilizes and the world could become a more dangerous place.

If the economy works and grows and there is opportunity for everyone, most other issues will fall into place, and there will be economic resources to address those that do not. This book focuses on an economic solution to the problem of falling standards of living of over half the workers in the USA.

Although based on an analysis of the United States economy, most of the material in the book applies to all of the Western democracies.

4. Other Perspectives

Numerous books have been written on the subject of income inequality. Two prominent books are *Capitalism in the Twenty-First Century* by Thomas Piketty and *Saving Capitalism for the Many, Not the Few*, by Robert Reich. Both books are excellent, and are important resources for understanding the issues.

Thomas Piketty argues that the divergence between the rich and the rest began when tax rates for the rich began to fall, and that as a result the rate of return on capital became greater than economic growth, leading to increasing wealth disparity. He argues that there is a correlation between falling tax rates and wealth divergence, and he concludes that low taxes for the rich are the cause. The evidence he presents is sound, but the conclusion he draws from it is not complete. Correlation does not necessarily imply causation. Falling taxes for the rich is not the root cause of income inequality. Piketty advocates raising taxes on the rich and taxing capital as a solution. Raising taxes on the rich will make the rich poorer, and it may make the poor richer, but it will not make the middle class richer.

Robert Reich is a professor at the University of California Berkley and he was the Secretary of Labor under Bill Clinton. He argues that the reason for the increasing wealth gap is that the rich have used their political influence to have the laws and taxes changed to favor themselves. Reich also advocates taxing the rich more, and using the proceeds to pay for education and assistance for the poor.

Taxing the rich to provide more services and income support for the poor is a form of income redistribution. *Income participation* as advocated in this book is a more constructive way to improve the incomes and standards of living for low and middle income workers than income redistribution.

5. The Golden Age of Capitalism

It hasn't always been this way. For many years all income categories experienced rapid improvement in their living standards. Post World War II, from 1945 until 1970, the USA and the Western economies experienced a "Golden Age of Capitalism" characterized by rapid economic growth, high productivity growth, rapidly rising GDP per capita, and increasing wages. The middle class expanded rapidly, as did their standard of living.

Keynesian economics was the predominant economic theory of the Golden Age. There were many economic influences during this time, including bouts of high inflation, an oil crisis, recessions, the Korean War (1950-53) and the Vietnam War (1955-75), but the overall economic trend was very positive.

The Golden Age of Capitalism had three major economic characteristics that were the key to the rapid growth. Trade was a small part of the economy and the USA ran a small trade surplus. There was rapid productivity growth during this era. Low income, middle income and high income wages all tracked productivity growth, resulting in an expanding middle class and rapid growth in standards of living for all.

6. Productivity Trends

As shown in Figure 6.1, Labor Productivity has increased continuously since WWII. It has averaged around 2 percent, with periods where it has been substantially higher, and periods when it has been down to just over 1 percent. During the Golden Age of Capitalism from 1947 to 1973 it averaged 2.8 percent per year.

Figure 6-1 Chart of Productivity and Hourly Compensation Change by Year

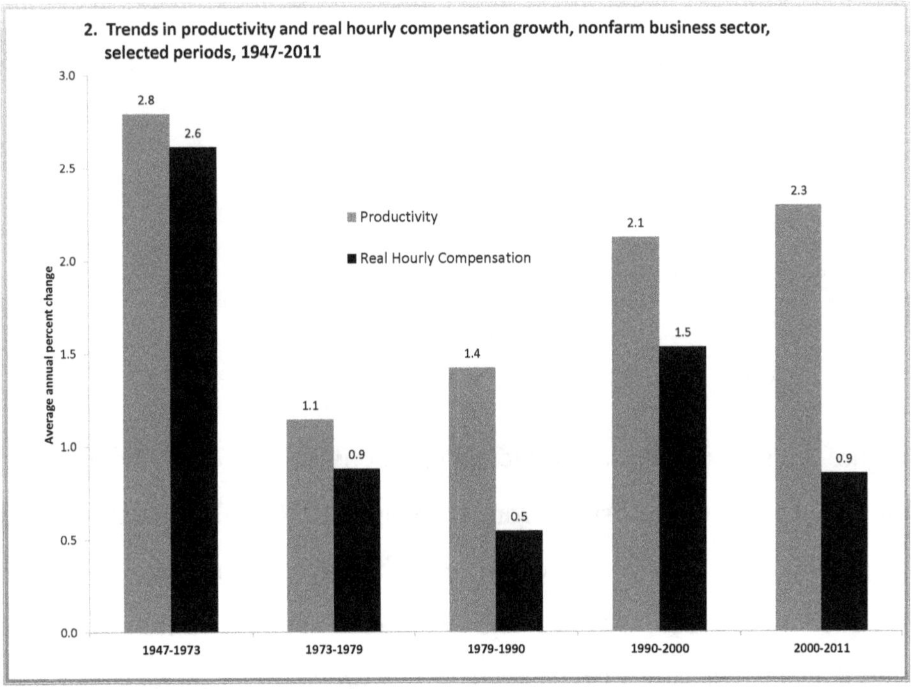

2. Trends in productivity and real hourly compensation growth, nonfarm business sector, selected periods, 1947-2011

Source: US Bureau of Labor Statistics [4]

The average productivity gain since 2000 has been 1.95 percent. [5] Compensation has not tracked productivity since 1973.

Productivity Economics

Figure 6-2 Chart of Wages and Productivity by Year

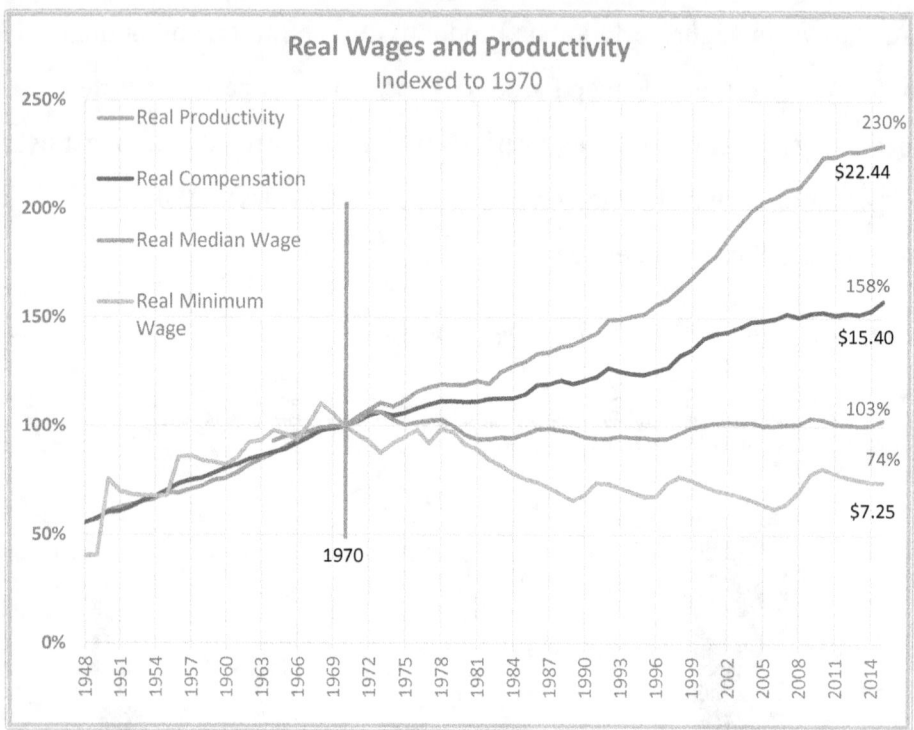

Source: Federal Reserve Bank of St Louis.[6]

Figure 6.2 shows that wages tracked productivity very closely during the Golden Age of Capitalism. From 1948 until 1970 real productivity and wages increased by 84 percent. Something happened around 1970. Productivity improvements and workers' compensation diverged dramatically. Between 1970 and 2015 real productivity increased by 130 percent but the real minimum wage decreased by 26%, the real median wage only increased by 3 percent, and real compensation only increased by 58 percent.

Making Capitalism Work Again

The US minimum wage increased in nominal and real terms until 1968, then leveled off until 1978, and it has fallen in real terms ever since. If the US federal minimum wage had tracked productivity since 1970 it would have been $22.44 in 2015 instead of $7.25. The median wage would be $1860 per week instead of $806. The lowest-earning 50 percent of workers have not seen any of the benefits of the growth of the economy since 1970. This is the primary reason for the declining middle class standard of living. In contrast the return on capital far exceeds productivity growth. The total real return including dividends for the S&P 500 has been over 1000% since 1970.

If wages had tracked productivity since 1970, US GDP would be much higher because consumption and investment would be much higher. Government revenues would also be much higher which would support increased infrastructure and social spending.

Figure 6-3 Chart of Family Income Growth pre and post 1970

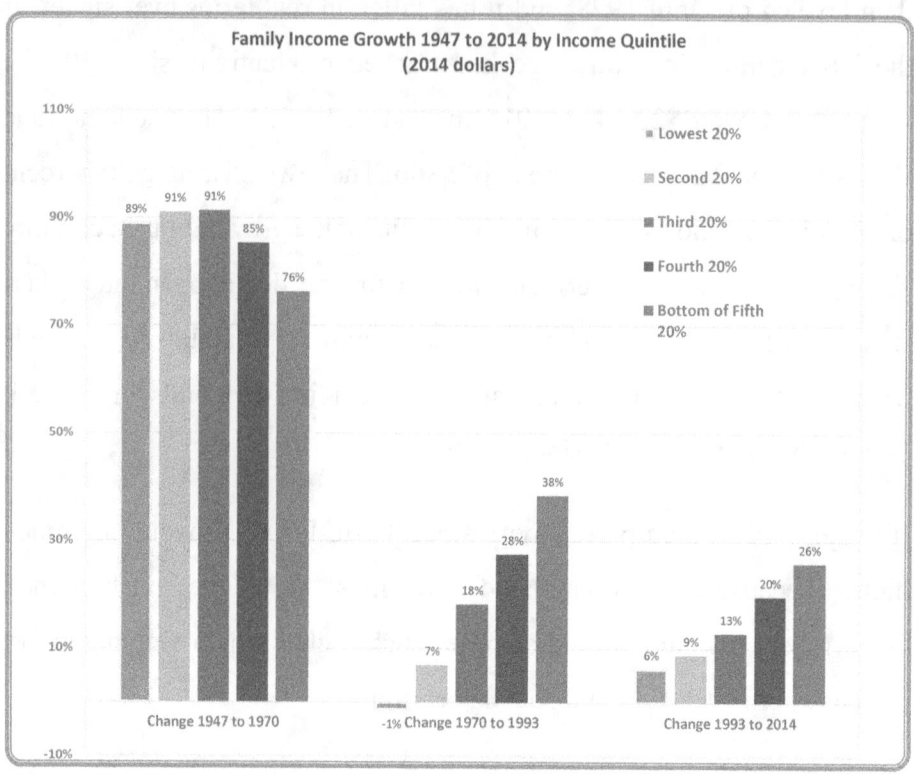

Source: US Census Bureau Table F1

Figure 6.3 shows that during the Golden Age of Capitalism from 1947 until around 1970 the benefits of productivity improvement applied equally across the wage spectrum. Everybody had remarkable growth in their standard of living. Incomes went up by 91 percent for middle income groups, 89 percent for low income and 76 percent for high income groups over a period of 23 years. Everybody became much wealthier.

From 1970 until 2014 the increase in family income was much less. One important thing to note is that post 1970 everybody, including high-income earners up to the 95th income percentile, did much worse than in the 1947 to 1970 Golden Age period despite similar productivity improvements over each of the periods. If incomes do not track productivity improvements, every income group loses, except the ultra-rich who do not work for wages.

Note that there is some discrepancy in the numbers in Figures 6-1 to 6-3 because the data comes from different sources and they differ slightly, however they all clearly indicate the same trends.

7. The End of the Golden Age of Capitalism

There is not a consensus among economists as to what caused the Golden Age of Capitalism to end.

A number of significant economic events happened in the 1970 time frame, including the introduction of personal computers, the oil crisis, the collapse of the Bretton Woods system, and the displacement of Keynesian economics by monetarist economics.

I believe that the major cause of the end of the Golden Age of Capitalism was the collapse of the Bretton Woods system, which resulted in the US dollar becoming the world's reserve currency.

Bretton Woods

> The Bretton Woods system of monetary management established the rules for commercial and financial relations among the United States, Canada, Western Europe, Australasia and Japan in the mid-20th century. The Bretton Woods system was the first example of a fully negotiated monetary order intended to govern monetary relations among independent nation-states. The chief features of the Bretton Woods system were an obligation for each country to adopt a monetary policy that maintained the exchange rate ($\pm$ 1 per cent) by tying its currency to gold and the ability of the IMF to bridge temporary imbalances of payments. Also, there was a need to address the lack of cooperation among other countries and to prevent competitive devaluation of the currencies as well.

Making Capitalism Work Again

On 15 August 1971, the United States unilaterally terminated convertibility of the US dollar to gold, effectively bringing the Bretton Woods system to an end and rendering the dollar a fiat currency. This action, referred to as the Nixon shock, created the situation in which the US dollar became a reserve currency used by many states. At the same time, many fixed currencies (such as the pound sterling, for example) also became free-floating.[7]

The end of Bretton Woods introduced the "Triffin Dilemma".

The Triffin Dilemma

It was understood by many leading economists, including John Maynard Keynes, that the demise of Bretton Woods would create a serious problem called the "Triffin Dilemma," named after the Belgian economist who first described the problem.

The essence of the Triffin Dilemma is that nations need to accumulate currency reserves in order to provide stability for their own currencies and economies. This means that the nation that provides the reserve currency must run trade deficits in order to allow other nations to accumulate currency reserves.

The collapse of the Bretton Woods system and the adoption of the US dollar as the world reserve currency dictated that the USA must run perpetual trade deficits. In other words, the USA has a *"mandated trade deficit."*

Productivity Economics

As described in the following chapters, running significant trade deficits makes it mathematically impossible for national wage growth to track national productivity growth. Instead, national wages, especially unskilled wages, are coupled to world labor demand/supply rather than domestic demand/supply. This was a major factor leading to the end of the Golden Age of Capitalism.

Another serious long-term impact of the Triffin Dilemma is that the US Federal Reserve cannot effectively regulate the US economic cycle, since the whole demand side of the national GDP equation has become a world issue rather than a domestic issue.

As a result of the collapse of Bretton Woods, no nation can effectively regulate its own economy and there is no agency that has effective oversight of the world economy. The world economy is entirely laissez-faire. This creates significant risk of worldwide instability or perhaps even a worldwide depression.

8. The Fundamental Root Causes

The problems of low economic growth and declining middle class incomes have four fundamental root causes that are interdependent.

The first root cause is that US labor productivity gains are not effectively coupled to the economy and they are not distributed in a manner that benefits the economy.

The second root cause is the US trade deficit in goods and services.

The third root cause is that the US Federal Reserve (Central Bank) does not have an effective means to stimulate the economy when it is demand constrained.

The fourth root cause is the way US corporations are taxed.

9. The Trade Deficit Problem

Trade is the exchange of goods or services. Trade by definition is balanced and it enriches all participants. It is win/win. The more trade there is, the better for all parties.

The exchange of goods for debt is not trade, it is a transfer of wealth and a transfer of productivity gains. It is win/lose and it enriches the exporter and the rentiers at the expense of the importer. Much of what passes for trade today falls into this category.

Economists argue that the system is self-regulating and that over time things will automatically come into balance due to currency adjustments. The Triffin Dilemma and over forty years of history suggests otherwise. In any case, the system can be gamed for very long periods of time, as China is doing today and Japan and Korea did before them. A great deal of damage to people and economies can be done in the meantime. It is possible to eliminate an entire industry that has a natural competitive advantage by gaming the system for sufficiently long. It is also possible to demote much of the middle class if the trade deficit continues for long enough.

Many large US corporations offshore much of their manufacturing, and increasingly many of their services such as customer support. The Chinese are not causing the US trade deficit and US unemployment. Rather, it is US corporations who are acting in their own economic interest. The US government has created an environment where the economically prudent thing is to produce offshore.

Making Capitalism Work Again

China did not decide to manufacture your iPhone, your TV, your furniture, and your clothes in China. That decision was made by the major corporations who control the intellectual property and the channels to market, but it is not their fault either.

Corporations are amoral and simply do what makes economic sense within the law and trade agreements. The large US trade deficit is a result of failed government policy and the world trade imbalances are the result of failed WTO, IMF, and G20 policy.

The US has a trade deficit of over 3 percent of GDP per year. This is more than its productivity or GDP growth.

10. Economic Stimulation Problem

The second root cause of low economic growth and declining middle class incomes is that the US Federal Reserve (central bank) or any other nation's central bank, does not have an effective means to stimulate the economy when demand is too low or GDP growth is below the target rates.

The lack of effective mechanisms to stimulate the economy and employment when the normal methods of interest rate adjustments and money supply have reached their limits, has caused the low-income and middle classes to fall behind. The federal government or the Federal Reserve (central banks) have no direct way to stimulate employment.

The central bank and the government use interest rates, money supply, government spending and infrastructure programs to regulate the economy, but they do not and cannot work. Interest rates have primarily been used as a means to control inflation and they have an indirect effect on employment, but as rates approach zero, it is like pushing on a string. You do not need to be a control engineer to understand that it is impossible to control a system with many degrees of freedom using just one control parameter, but that is what is being attempted. It is like trying to fly an airplane using only the throttle.

This problem has existed in Japan since they went into recession in 1991.[8] Japan has been suffering from deflation or stagnation ever since. They have tried everything: low interest rates, monetary stimulation, and increased government spending, but nothing works. They still have stagflation or deflation, further compounded by the world's highest debt levels. For the Japanese there is no easy way out. Now much of Europe and the Americas is following down the same perilous path.

11. Negative Interest Rates

The Federal Reserve's use of money supply and interest rates to stimulate the economy has caused interest rates to become so low that they are below the rate of inflation, so real interest rates have become negative. Interest rates are so low because interest rates and money supply are the only tools available to the US Federal Reserve. When the economy requires stimulation, the Reserve Bank lowers rates and/or prints money even if this results in negative real interest rates.

Negative real interest rates, where the interest rate is lower than the inflation rate, destroys wealth. If you put enough money in the bank to buy 100 loaves of bread, then a year later you take it out and you only have enough to buy 95 loaves, then some of your wealth has been destroyed. An economy that destroys wealth as a matter of policy is not working for the people. In reality, wealth hasn't been destroyed, it has just been transferred to others.

Negative real interest rates penalize savers, the retired, pension plans and wealth creators, while they reward speculators, debtors, churners, irresponsible governments, and bankers. It is a government endorsed and sponsored transfer of wealth from the middle class to the rich. These low rates are doing serious damage to the economy.

Large banks, large corporations and wealthy people are making a great deal of money at the expense of the taxpayer because they are the only ones who have access to the subsidized, below cost funds created by the Federal Reserve. This activity does not create much employment or economic growth but it does increase the wealth of the One Percent. Negative real interest rates have helped the One Percent prosper and the rest of society to fall behind.

12.   The Corporate Income Tax Problem

The way corporate income is taxed in the USA is another root cause of low economic growth and declining middle class incomes. It creates an uneven playing field for domestic producers and provides an incentive for US companies to produce goods and services offshore. Obviously this is not good for the US economy.

With the present regime of taxes on corporate profits, a US corporation pays US income tax on products that it sells in Ireland. An Irish company pays Irish income tax on products they sell in the USA. However, the US tax rate is 39 percent, and the Irish rate is 12.5 percent, so the Irish company has a large advantage.

Many countries have realized the importance of this and have substantially reduced their corporate income tax rate. The US and Japan have the highest corporate income tax rates in the G20.

Figure 12-1 shows the federal corporate tax rates and the federal GST rates for various countries.

Making Capitalism Work Again

Figure 12-1 Table of Corporate Tax and GST Rates by Country

Country	2015 Corp tax rate %	2015 GST rate		Country	2015 Corp tax rate %	2015 GST rate
USA	35	0%		Sweden	22	25% *
France	34.43	20% *		Finland	20	24% *
Belgium	33	21% *		Iceland	20	24% *
Australia	30	10%		Turkey	20	18% *
Mexico	30	16%		UK	20	20% *
New Zeal	28	15%		Czech	19	21% *
Portugal	28	23% *		Hungary	19	27% *
Spain	28	21% *		Poland	19	23% *
Italy	27.5	22% *		Germany	15.8	19% *
Norway	27	25% *		Canada	15	5%
Israel	26.5	17% *		Ireland	12.5	23% *
Greece	26	23% *		Switzer	8.5	8% *
Austria	25	20%		China	25	17% *
Netherlnd	25	21% *		Russia	20	0-18%
Japan	23.9	17.5		Singapore	17	7%
Denmark	23.5	25%		Caymans	0	22% *
Korea	22	10%				

Source: OECD [9]

* In many countries the GST may be lower for some essential goods and services, and many countries have state GSTs that are added to the federal GST. The state tax component is not shown in this table.

Corporate tax rates vary in some countries depending on the industry and company size. Many countries including the USA also have state taxes that are added to the federal tax. State taxes are excluded in this table, but states that have an additional corporate income tax compound the problem.

In fact, most US companies are not actually paying US income tax on foreign sales. They do not have to pay the tax until they repatriate the foreign income back to the US, so they defer indefinitely. Apple has over $181 billion in retained profits in offshore accounts that they will not bring back to the US because of the tax implications. Large US corporations have over $2.1 trillion in deferred taxes sitting in offshore accounts.[10] That is US domestic investment that is being blocked by a shockingly bad tax policy.[11]

This tax disparity is even causing US companies to undertake reverse mergers to move their official corporate headquarters and tax residency to low tax regimes. The latest is Pfizer who are merging with Allergan (a much smaller Irish company) to become an Irish company. Johnson Controls is also planning to do a reverse merger with Tyco. Tyco is a much smaller Irish company.[12, 13] Don't blame the companies, blame your government for not doing their job to protect the interests of US citizens and US corporations.

Minimal US income taxes are paid on most products imported to and sold in the US. Most of the profits are recorded in low tax jurisdictions. It is perfectly legal.

13. The Labor Productivity Problem

The most important core problem is the way productivity gains are distributed in the economy.

> Productivity isn't everything, but in the long run it is almost everything. A country's ability to improve its standard of living over time depends almost entirely on its ability to raise its output per worker. (Paul Krugman)[14]

The way productivity growth is coupled to the economy is everything else.

Labor productivity is defined as "output per unit of labor."[15]

Labor productivity in the US has historically increased by over 2 percent per year. Some years it has increased over 3 percent. Since 2008 it has increased by an average of 1.3 percent per year.

That means each worker generates on average 1 or 2 percent more goods or services per hour per year compounded. It is not because workers have worked harder or longer. Productivity improvements are generally the result of increased automation, better materials, better processes or better tools.

To illustrate, let's consider a hypothetical nation that has a constant population and a closed market with no external trade.

If labor productivity goes up 2 percent and prices remain the same and nobody gets a raise, then workers work 2 percent less and hence get paid

2 percent less to supply the market. Demand will go down by 2 percent since workers are the consumers and they have 2 percent less money to spend. Tax revenues go down so the government has less money to spend. GDP goes down.

If prices are reduced because the productivity increase lowers costs, wages and GDP will still go down.

The only way around this problem is to increase demand by more than the labor productivity improvement.

Gross domestic product (GDP) is the monetary value of all the finished goods and services produced within a country's borders. There are several ways of calculating GDP, all of which should have the same result. I will use the expenditure method.

GDP is the sum of consumption (C), investment (I), government spending (G) and net exports (X – M).[16]

GDP = C + I + G + (X – M)

If trade is balanced and X = M then GDP = C + I + G

Given a government constrained by excessive deficits and debt, and a stable trade balance, GDP cannot increase unless (C), the purchasing power of consumers, increases or investment (I) increases. Increased investment or increased government spending can cause GDP to rise, but without increased demand, there is no reason to invest to increase production, and government spending is constrained by excessive debt burdens. It all hinges on the consumer.

Consumer spending C represents over 70 percent of US GDP.[17] Consumer spending has been increasing slowly but that is primarily because of increasing employment and expanding credit caused by low interest rates. Increasing credit driven by increasing incomes and modest inflation is sustainable provided that debt ratios remain reasonable. Increasing credit driven by decreasing interest rates given stagnant incomes is an unsustainable bubble that will ultimately collapse with unfavorable results. The US is nearing full employment so increasing employment cannot drive increasing consumer spending much longer unless wages rise.

The *only* sustainable way to constantly increase consumer purchasing power is to pass productivity increases on to workers as increased wages.

14. Productivity Case Study

Figure 14.1 examines what happens if there is a 2 percent productivity increase and how it effects the economy if all or only part of that productivity increase is passed on as an increase in wages. It assumes that similar compensation decisions are being made throughout the entire economy.

It is presented as a base case starting point and evaluation of what happens if wages are increased by 0 percent (Case A), 1 percent (Case B), 2 percent (Case C) (the full productivity increase), 3 percent (Case D) and 4 percent (Case E).

The example assumes the workers have a $10 per hour wage for the base case.

For the base case, it takes 10 hours to build one unit, and the units sold is set at an arbitrary value of 1000. For cases A to E hours worked are adjusted to reflect the productivity improvement.

This chart assumes that sales volumes (units sold) are modestly elastic, so sales volumes change in proportion to hours worked. In other words, the product is not an essential product where sales would not change even if wages decrease, nor is it a totally discretionary product that people will stop buying if wages decrease.

The price/unit is set to $300 for the base case and held constant unless costs increase. Cost per unit = 90 percent of price/unit, assuming a 10 percent profit for the base case then adjusted for the productivity and wage increase for the other cases. Profit = price - cost.

For each case wages, costs, and profits are adjusted to reflect the impact of the 2 percent productivity improvement and the wage increase.

Figure 14-1 Productivity Case Study Table

CASE	BASE	Case A	Case B	Case C	Case D	Case E
Productivity Increase	CASE	2%	2%	2%	2%	2%
Wage increase		0%	1%	2%	3%	4%
Worker Hourly wage	$ 10.00	$ 10.00	$ 10.10	$ 10.20	$ 10.30	$ 10.40
Units Sold	1,000	980	990	1,000	1,010	1,020
Hours worked	10,000	9,604	9,702	9,800	9,898	9,996
Actual Wages paid	$ 100,000	$ 96,040	$ 97,990	$ 99,960	$ 101,949	$ 103,958
Price per unit	$ 300.00	$ 300.00	$ 300.00	$ 300.00	$ 303.00	$ 306.00
Cost per unit	$ 270.00	$ 264.60	$ 267.30	$ 270.00	$ 272.70	$ 275.40
Profit per unit	$ 30.00	$ 35.40	$ 32.70	$ 30.00	$ 30.30	$ 30.60
Total Sales	$ 300,000	$ 294,000	$ 297,000	$ 300,000	$ 306,030	$ 312,120
Total Profit $$	$ 30,000	$ 34,692	$ 32,373	$ 30,000	$ 30,603	$ 31,212
Profit % of sales	10%	12%	11%	10%	10%	10%
Effect on total employment hours		-4.0%	-3.0%	-2.0%	-1.0%	0.0%
Effect on actual wages paid		-4.0%	-2.0%	-0.04%	1.9%	4.0%
Effect on Inflation		0.0%	0.0%	0.0%	1.0%	2.0%
Effect on profit		15.6%	7.9%	0.0%	2.0%	4.0%
Effect on National GDP		-2.0%	-1.0%	0.0%	2.0%	4.0%

The results are interesting and informative. Study the table carefully. It is the key to understanding this book.

Case A: none of the productivity gain is passed on to the workers as wages so their actual hours and wages decline by 4 percent because they work fewer hours to produce the same output, and the sales have decreased because their hours have decreased, so unemployment increases. GDP falls, but profits increase substantially despite the sales decrease. There is no impact on inflation providing that companies do not have to reduce prices. For companies this is good in the short term because profits increase, but if it is done year after year volumes keep declining and eventually it stops working. For corporate executives receiving performance based pay and short-term shareholders, this is a good outcome. For everyone else this is a bad outcome. If companies are forced to reduce prices due to competition or falling demand, there is deflation and everything is even worse.

Case B: the workers are given an increase of half the increase in productivity. This has a similar result. Sales decrease, worker hours and wages decrease, profits increase over the base case, GDP falls, and there is no effect on inflation.

Case C: the workers are given all of the productivity increase of 2 percent. Sales hold steady versus the base case. Workers' wages return to near the initial level but hours are still less because they are producing more units per hour. Profits are the same as the base case. There is no effect on inflation or GDP.

Case D: wages are increased 3 percent, which is 1 percent higher than productivity growth. This causes GDP and profits to grow but it causes mild inflation. Note that the workers are earning more but they are still working fewer hours, thus contributing to unemployment or perhaps a shorter workweek.

Case E: giving a 4 percent raise causes 4 percent GDP and profit growth, but it only causes 2 percent inflation. These are the Fed targets for GDP growth and inflation. Workers are earning more and total hours worked are back to the base case. All in all, this is the *perfect* outcome.

Productivity Economics

If wage growth is greater than productivity growth, then employment increases since demand grows by more than the employment reduction caused by the productivity increase.

If the benefits of increased worker productivity are coupled back into the economy via increasing workers' wages, the economy grows at its maximum potential. If they are not, economic growth is far below optimal.

The problem is that passing the benefits of increased productivity on to workers is a "*Prisoner's Dilemma*" situation. If all companies pass on the productivity gain, everyone benefits, and the economy prospers, but if any one company capitulates to the pressure to increase short-term profits by retaining the productivity gain, then all their competitors must do the same or they will be at a competitive disadvantage. However, if none of the companies pass on the productivity gains, everybody is worse off. [18]

The benefits of productivity gains can only be realized if all companies are required to share the gains with all labor. That can only happen through government action, or if there is significant competition for labor, especially unskilled labor.

It is unlikely that there will ever be sufficient competition for unskilled labor to drive up wages at the same rate as productivity like there was in the Golden Age of Capitalism, for reasons explained in the following chapters, so that leaves government action as the only alternative.

Making Capitalism Work Again

The Government must increase the national minimum wage by at least the national productivity gain every year, otherwise it creates a falling standard of living for workers, stagnant demand and deflationary pressure.

Productivity coupling, where wages are linked to national productivity growth, creates *income participation* where all workers participate in the growing wealth of the nation, and it causes productivity increases to translate into increased demand, increased sales, increased investment and increased profits, as occurred during the Golden Age of Capitalism.

However, there is a Catch 22. "Productivity coupling" is not possible unless there is "mandated balanced trade."

As shown in the following chapters, unless there is "*mandated balanced trade,*" even if productivity gains are passed on to the workers as wage increases, most of the gain will leak offshore to lower wage jurisdictions and the economic benefits will be lost.

If trade is not balanced, national GDP growth is constrained by world demand growth. This is why US GDP growth is so low despite reasonable US productivity growth. It is constrained by world consumption growth and the portion that US producers can capture. If you do not have "*mandated balanced trade,*" nations are not masters of their own economy or destiny.

If there is "*mandated balanced trade,*" national GDP growth is only constrained by growth in domestic supply and demand, which is constrained by national wage growth. National wage growth is constrained by national productivity growth.

The optimum for the nation, for workers' standards of living, and even for capitalists whose income depends on increasing revenues and profits, is to set wage growth higher than productivity growth.

With *mandated balanced trade*, national GDP growth is only constrained by how fast you can grow national productivity and incomes.

If the average national wage growth is lower than productivity growth, then GDP cannot grow faster than world consumption growth since domestic consumption cannot increase.

There is abundant evidence that the USA is in a Case A or B scenario. GDP is stagnant but profits are growing. Profits are at historically high levels and are still growing, albeit at a slowing rate, just as Case A predicts. Domestic sales and revenue growth for many companies is stagnant or even negative. Productivity has increased over 11 percent since 2007. Large corporations maintain or increase production every year, and they lay off workers every year. Median income wages have been declining. There is no reason for companies to reinvest domestically because there is no opportunity to increase sales domestically and there are tax and cost incentives to produce offshore to satisfy any increase in international demand and even for increases in domestic demand.

For companies, the status quo (Case A or B) is that all else being equal (trade, money supply, credit, population, employment, demographics etc.)

consumption growth must be less than productivity growth. "If wage growth (wg) is less than productivity growth (pg) then consumption growth (cg) is less than productivity growth." **If wg<pg then cg<pg**. Falling wages also results in falling credit which causes negative feedback.

Productivity growth is like the force of gravity in physics. It is a relatively weak economic force however it is cumulative so over time and distance it always dominates. The Federal Reserve regulates money supply and interest rates which are strong forces over the short term but they cannot compensate for the overwhelming effects of productivity increases over the long term. Long term productivity increases without *productivity coupling* acts as a deterrent to consumption growth and hence economic growth.

GDP=C+I+G+(X-M). Consumption (C) accounts for over 70 percent of GDP so consumption growth (cg) is the major determinant of long term GDP growth trends.

With *productivity coupling* productivity increases act as a stimulant to economic growth. With *productivity coupling* "if wage growth is greater than productivity growth then consumption growth is greater than productivity growth long term." **If wg>pg then cg>pg** over the long term. Increasing wages also causes increasing credit and increasing consumption drives investment both of which provide positive economic feedback.

Productivity Economics

Consumption growth (cg) may be larger or smaller than wage growth (wg) in the short term due to influences such as credit changes, demographic or employment changes etc. but long term productivity growth and *productivity coupling* are the dominant factors.

Wage growth has been decoupled from productivity growth for forty-six years (since 1970). Forty-six years is enough time for the weak force to dominate. The weak economy is the result. If wage growth had tracked productivity growth since 1973 consumption (C) would be between 60 and 100 percent higher than it is today and there would be solid economic growth. No amount of fiscal stimulation can compensate for a sixty plus percent loss of consumption capacity.

For corporate America there is a choice between the status quo with stagnant revenues, falling expenses and increasing profits, or *productivity coupling* and increasing revenues, increasing expenses and increasing profits. Which is better? There is no future in the status quo. Stagnant revenues are not good for corporate America. The stock market speaks very clearly on this. Companies with growing revenues are valued much more highly than companies with falling or stagnant revenues. Profit is less important than revenue growth for stock valuation.

"Collectively, American businesses currently have $1.9 trillion in cash. Not only is this state of affairs unparalleled in economic history ... corporations have traditionally been borrowers not savers."[19]

Companies are returning retained earnings through share buy-backs and dividends at record rates. Things are so out of whack that companies are borrowing the cheap funds provided by the Federal Reserve to return capital to their shareholders rather than soliciting money from investors as they would in a normal growing economy. The problem is stagnant demand. The US economy and most Western economies are trapped in a Case A or B situation.

The Federal Reserve is flooding the market with cheap money hoping it will increase spending, but it is not increasing spending or investment and it is not increasing inflation as traditional economic theory predicts. That is because all that money is only available to rich people and companies with good credit ratings and they are already awash in cash needing a home.

> One rule which woe betides the banker who fails to heed it … Never lend any money to anybody unless they don't need it. –
>
> Ogden Nash

The stagnant demand caused by falling incomes and the trade imbalance has also caused productivity growth to stall. Productivity growth is driven by investment and with the present economy there is little reason to invest in America.

The only solution is to increase demand from workers, and that can only be done by increasing wages.

Politicians who promise to accelerate economic growth without addressing the four fundamental root causes are blowing smoke. It is mathematically impossible to achieve US growth rates that exceed world demand growth without implementing *"mandated balanced trade"* and a mechanism whereby the national minimum wage increases by at least the same rate as productivity.

In the Golden Age of Capitalism, between WWII and 1970, by happy circumstance rather than good planning, we had the right conditions where trade was not a major part of the economy, productivity increased rapidly, and productivity increases were shared with the workers because of strong unions and labor shortages. There was a virtuous circle of increasing productivity, increasing wages, increasing demand, increasing profits and increasing government revenue.

If you want to improve the wellbeing of the workers, you must maximize productivity growth and share the benefits of productivity improvements with the workers. Workers need Case D or E.

If you want to improve the wellbeing of companies and the owners of capital (the rich and your pension fund), you must ensure that there is continuous revenue and profit growth. Companies need increasing revenues and profits to thrive and to please their shareholders. Capitalists need Case D or E. That is the only way they get a long-term payback on the investment they made to achieve the productivity gain. Government needs a growing economy to service debt and to provide ongoing social services.

Taxing capital as proposed by Thomas Piketty does not maximize productivity growth. It reduces investment, which reduces productivity growth. It will not create wealth or long-term increases in the standard of living for the middle class. It is just redistribution.

15. The Effect of Trade for Debt

Figure 15-1 US Trade Balance Graph

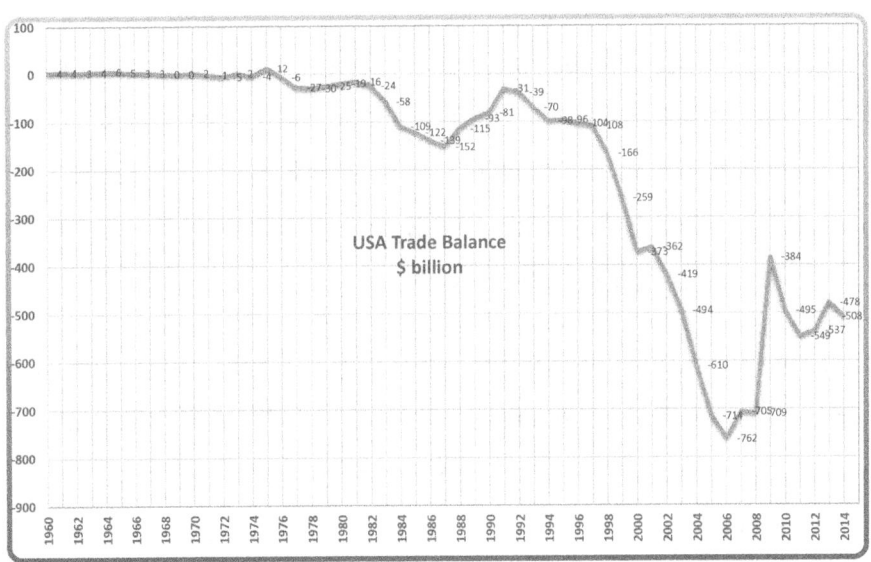

Source: US Census Data.[20]

As shown in Figure 15-1, In the early 1970s, due to the collapse of Bretton Woods the US trade balance began to trend negative, and it has been increasingly negative ever since. Prior to 1970 there was a modest trade surplus. By 2005 the deficit had reached over $700 billion and it is still trending around $500 billion, which is over 3 percent of GDP.

The large trade deficit has had a major impact. It is the key.

The previous chapter showed that productivity growth, and how the benefits of productivity growth are distributed, is critical to economic growth. Trade has an important effect on productivity growth and *productivity coupling*.

Trade enhances productivity because the aggregate output per unit of labor increases through the magic of "comparative advantage." True trade increases productivity.

Consider the example shown in Figure 15-2 where two tradesmen make desks and chairs. Tradesman A has specialized tools for making chairs so he can produce 25 chairs per week but only 20 desks per week. Tradesman B has specialized tools for producing desks so he can produce 25 desks per week but only 20 chairs per week.

Over a 2-week period alternating between desks and chairs Tradesman A can produce 25 chairs and 20 desks for a total of 45 units. If the market price for a table or chair is $100, then Tradesman A can produce $4,500 worth of product in 2 weeks. Tradesman B produces 20 chairs and 25 desks worth $4,500 in 2 weeks.

If they specialize and Tradesman A focuses on building chairs, he can produce 50 chairs valued at $5,000 in two weeks. His output has gone up by $500. Tradesman B builds only desks. His output increase due to specialization is also $500. Together they have produced 5 more desks and 5 more chairs.

Figure 15-2 Comparative Advantage Trade Example

Without Specialization

	Production capacity Chairs/ week	Production capacity Desks/ week	2 weeks total production Desks & Chairs	2 weeks production
Tradesman A	25	20	45	$ 4,500
Tradesman B	20	25	45	$ 4,500
Total			90	$ 9,000

With Specialization A specializes in Chairs. B in Desks

	Chairs/ week	Desks/ week	2 weeks production specializing	
Tradesman A	25	0	50	$ 5,000
Tradesman B	0	25	50	$ 5,000
Total			100	$ 10,000
Productivity Gain			11.1%	

Post Balanced Trade

	Desks	Chairs	Value	
Tradesman A	25	25	$ 5,000	
Tradesman B	25	25	$ 5,000	

Post Trade For Debt

	Desks	Chairs	Value	Debt
Tradesman A	30	25	$ 5,500	(500)
Tradesman B	20	25	$ 4,500	

Now suppose they trade desks and chairs so that each ends up with half the production. Tradesman A and B each end up with 25 desks and 25 chairs. Both have benefited. Overall productivity increased 11 percent.

Productivity Economics

This is why trade is beneficial. *Comparative advantage* benefits all parties by allowing them to concentrate on what they are best at. It is a way to enhance productivity. It is win/win.

Now let's see what happens when Tradesman B decides that he only needs the 20 desks he was able to make before trading, and that he will let Tradesman A owe him for the 5 desk difference—in other words, trade for debt.

Now B has 20 desks, 25 chairs, and an IOU for 5 x $100 = $500.

Tradesman A has 30 desks instead of 25 and he owes B $500. On paper he is no worse off. His assets offset his liabilities. However, he needs to sell the surplus desks or cut back production by 5 desks. If he cuts production, then his productivity gain is gone. He is now only working 9 days out of 10. If there is balanced trade there will be a market for his extra desks somewhere, but if trade is not balanced and his country runs a trade deficit, it is like musical chairs: someone in the country will be left with less work.

Note that Tradesman B still reaps the enhanced productivity benefits. He has not had to cut his hours or production and he realizes the productivity gain caused by specialization. The benefits of the productivity enhancement from specialization have been transferred from A to B. A is the USA. B is China.

Balanced trade allows comparative advantage to be turned into a productivity gain for both parties. It is win/win.

Trade for debt negates any gains from *comparative advantage* for the country running a trade deficit. Trade for debt costs jobs and GDP growth. It is a transfer of productivity gains, jobs and wealth. It is win/lose.

The trade deficit is one of the major reasons that US wages have not tracked productivity gains since 1970.

Starting around 1971, trade became a significant factor in the US economy and the US worker began competing with overseas workers instead of trading with them. Overseas labor was substituted for US labor instead of trading labor to achieve *comparative advantage* through specialization. With trade for debt, what has essentially happened is that the US labor market has been unified with the world labor market.

With true trade workers utilize *comparative advantage* to increase their productivity, and all parties reap the benefits. With true trade domestic workers do not compete with offshore workers. Instead, they use comparative advantage to cooperate and specialize. It is win/win.

When you delve deeply into *comparative advantage* it becomes complicated and there are many things to consider, but there are some fundamental truths.

With "mandated balanced trade," jobs cannot be exported. Each nation is ring-fenced from a labor point of view. Each nation or common market must produce all it consumes (or the trade equivalent of all it consumes).

Productivity Economics

Nations should maximize trade to realize the significant productivity benefits of comparative advantage, but it must be balanced trade.

The trade imbalance is one of the major factors causing the decline of the low and middle income classes in America, and it is one of the major causes of the increasing wealth and income gaps.

With no restrictions on trade the unskilled labor market has essentially become infinite. The labor demand/supply curve that applies everywhere is the demand/supply curve for the world labor market, and since there is essentially an infinite supply of unskilled workers, all unskilled workers are stuck at the bottom of the curve.

That is not the intent of trade. The intent of trade is to achieve the benefits of *comparative advantage* for both parties. That means it must be true balanced trade, not trade for debt.

It is interesting to look at who wins and loses with unbalanced trade. Consider trade with China. The US consumer buys a consumer item that was made in China from a US retailer. That consumer article quickly depreciates to zero value. The consumer's wealth has gone down.

The US retailer bought the product from a Chinese manufacturer using US dollars. The US retailer and the Chinese manufacturer both make a profit on the sale.

The Chinese worker gets a job. The US worker has lost his job.

Making Capitalism Work Again

The Chinese manufacturer exchanges the US cash for Yuan currency at a Chinese government currency exchange.

The Chinese government then invests the US cash in US Treasuries to build up their currency reserves. They have an IOU that may ultimately be worthless.

The retailer's shareholders are wealthier. The bankers, lawyers and accountants who facilitated the international money flows all collect a commission. Wealth has been removed from the US worker's pocket, albeit voluntarily, and distributed to the Chinese worker and all the intermediary parties. The rich get richer. The poor lost their jobs and they got poorer.

As it stands presently, all G20 nations have ceded control of their economies to laissez-faire economics at a world scale (except perhaps China, which has a managed economy). The US Federal Reserve is effectively trying to regulate the world economy, not just the US economy, because the world's labor markets have been integrated and the US dollar is the dominant world reserve currency. The problem is that the Federal Reserve has neither the mandate nor the tools to regulate the world economy, so, as you would expect, it is not doing very well.

The lack of a world *"balanced trade mandate"* doesn't just affect the USA. Every nation is affected by the integration of world labor markets and the loss of the autonomy to regulate their own economies even if they have a trade surplus.

Productivity Economics

All other countries position their interest rates, money supply, labor rates and currencies relative to the US dollar. Now when the US or Europe prints money or changes interest rates, it is not just local to the US or Europe. The money floods the world.

With *mandated balanced trade*, common markets/currency areas are ring-fenced. They can set interest rates, wages, and money supply independently. They can control their economies independently and they are much less susceptible to economic disturbances in other countries.

The *balanced trade mandate* will change business mentality from a preference for producing in the lowest cost jurisdiction to a preference for producing goods and services in the regions where the markets are. This is already happening to some extent in automobile production.

Without balanced trade, money, products, services and labor services can all cross borders and the Federal Reserve has no control. The rich can follow the money. The rich own shares in multi-national corporations and benefit from increasing world demand and profits. They benefit if world demand and trade expand, regardless of location or balance. Workers and governments are tied to their country. They do not benefit from increasing international demand if trade is not balanced.

In order to prevent detractors pointing out the obvious flaw in this argument, the key exception needs to be addressed. It does make economic sense and it is beneficial for a nation to incur a trade deficit to import goods that will produce a productivity improvement.

For example, just as it makes sense for a company to incur debt to buy production machinery that will produce a future income stream, it makes sense for a country to incur debt to import capital equipment or Intellectual Property that will allow it to increase production and productivity. The key is that in both cases the capital investment must produce a future revenue stream. In other words, it must produce a future trade surplus. Clearly, this is not what the US is doing. It is mostly importing consumer goods that will not produce a future revenue stream or a future trade surplus.

To summarize, Trade for Debt has two serious consequences; it prevents the productivity gains of "comparative advantage" from being realized, and it effectively integrates domestic labor markets with international labor markets, thus preventing domestic wages from being coupled to domestic productivity gains. These two factors are the predominant reasons for the stagnation of middle and low-income wages and the growing income and wealth gaps.

16. Solutions

As discussed in the previous chapters, wages that are increasing slower than productivity growth, trade deficits, low interest rates, excessively low inflation, and inappropriate tax strategies have caused the US economy to substantially underperform its potential. This has caused low and middle income workers to fall behind. This has resulted in a falling standard of living for middle and low-income workers, and many economic, social and political problems.

The good news is that all these problems can be solved by making three changes:

1. Implement a balanced trade policy at the G20 or WTO level.
2. Change the Federal Reserve rules to disallow negative real interest rates and give the Federal Reserve the mandate to set the national minimum wage based on productivity gains.
3. Change the way corporations are taxed.

17. Solution 1: Mandated Balanced Trade

Mandated balanced trade can be implemented by having all G20 or WTO nations agree that any nation that has a goods and services trade surplus exceeding 1 percent of GDP must have zero import tariffs on all goods and services, without exception.

Any country with a trade deficit over 1 percent will set import duties equal to triple the deficit percent. The duties would be revised quarterly or even monthly. These duties would apply to all imported goods and services, including all energy products, uniformly and without exception. They would apply uniformly to all imports regardless of the country of origin. This would be phased in over a number of years to avoid a major shock to the world economy. Ideally, this should be done at the G20 or WTO level, but if this is not possible it could be implemented unilaterally by the USA and all countries with a trade deficit.

Note that this refers to the trade of all goods and services, including tourism, across borders. It does not refer to the Current Account. The Current Account includes other transactions such as investments, investment income, and foreign reserve transactions that are often far larger than the trade account, however Current Account imbalances do not have a direct effect on productivity gain realization or wages in the way trade imbalances do.

Mandated balanced trade does not mean that trade is balanced between each country; it means that the total trade for each country is balanced.

Productivity Economics

For example, the US may have a trade deficit with China but a trade surplus with other countries such that the trade balance is zero.

The balanced trade policy could allow counties with balanced trade to protect sectors that are critical to national security, such as food production, using tariffs of up to some agreed limit of around 10 percent maximum. The *balanced trade mandate* makes this economically inefficient for that country and would result in lower national wealth, but some countries may deem this appropriate and politically necessary. However, it would only be allowed if they have balanced trade.

18. Mandated Balanced Trade Effects

Mandated balanced trade changes everything.

Mandated balanced trade is different than trade that just happens to be balanced. *Mandated balanced trade* means that government regulatory agencies will take action to restore balance if trade becomes unbalanced. ***It is the belief and confidence that trade will remain balanced that causes companies and countries to change their behavior.***

Mandated balanced trade:

- makes government trade subsidies uneconomic. In a balanced trade regime, if you increase exports of one product by using subsidies, by definition you will decrease exports of some other products. Total exports are the same, but net profits and national income have been decreased by the amount of the subsidy. Subsidies have always been economic insanity, but this policy makes it obvious even to politicians.

- automatically causes countries to export their highest value added products and services. Exporting subsidized or low value products when you have a trade surplus reduces national wealth, government balance sheets and profits.

- provides incentives for countries to eliminate the numerous non-tariff trade barriers, since limiting imports of protected products prevents the export of higher value products.

- eliminates all tariffs and duties, and all the bureaucracy associated with them. All imports are taxed at the same rate. The rates

57

cannot be influenced by special interest or lobby groups. The invisible hand of the market decides everything else.

- eliminates the massive bureaucracy and expense required to negotiate, implement and enforce the current complex bilateral trade agreements. It reduces the size and cost of government. This is a productivity improvement. Note that it does not eliminate the need for trade agreements in areas such as intellectual property rights, applicable commercial law, product safely, child labor etc.

- stimulates world trade because it becomes obvious to everyone that trade is beneficial. If all trade is for *comparative advantage*, the more trade the better. Protectionist groups are discredited. This is particularly important during recessions when there is strong political pressure to curtail foreign imports.

- increases employment in all countries with a trade deficit. It may or may not reduce employment in countries with a trade surplus, depending on how they react to the new rules.

- increases government revenue in countries with a trade deficit so it reduces the fiscal deficit.

- provides a strong incentive for countries with a trade surplus to increase the value of their currency. This is the fastest and most efficient way to get to a balance. Their citizens will have more purchasing power and wealth.

- eliminates all incentives for currency devaluation. With *mandated balanced trade* you cannot increase exports or employment by devaluing your currency. Currency devaluations are one of the major destabilizing factors in the world economy. When a country starts to fall into recession, they devalue their currency in an attempt to stimulate exports and jobs to stabilize the situation. It is a beggar thy neighbor policy that tends to export instability. *Mandated balanced trade* eliminates the option of solving internal problems by stealing market share from another country. Now problems within a country must be addressed internally.

- provides an incentive for countries to maintain their currency at the highest level that sustains balanced trade. This maximizes purchasing power, standards of living, and national wealth. All developed countries would strive to have balanced trade, or a small trade deficit

Mandated balanced trade changes the way nations and corporations think.

Effectively, *mandated balanced trade* makes the whole world a free trade zone. It would be real trade based on comparative advantage, not trade based on who has the lowest labor rates. It is a trade policy designed to benefit both workers and the owners of capital.

Most importantly, mandated balanced trade:

- nationalizes productivity gains by preventing the benefits of productivity gains from being exported offshore. The countries with the highest rate of productivity improvement will have the largest increase in standard of living over time.

Productivity Economics

- makes it possible to couple wage growth to productivity improvements at a national level.

- effectively imposes the condition that each nation or common currency area must produce all it consumes or the trade equivalent thereof. It ring-fences national labor markets so that work cannot be moved offshore when domestic wages increase.

- Makes national minimum wage increases possible and highly beneficial.

19. Productivity Equilibrium Economics

Mandated balanced trade makes a new economic model possible.

From 1945 until 1971 the US economy was primarily regulated using Keynesian economic policies. Keynesian policies were largely demand-side economics. From 1971 Friedman monetarism policies and Reagan supply-side economics were predominant.

Now the US and the Western World economic policy should shift to a *"Productivity Equilibrium Economics"* model or perhaps it should be called *"Productivity Side Economics."*

The Principles of Productivity Equilibrium Economics

- Thou shalt maximize productivity growth.
- Thou shalt maintain equilibrium.
- The economic objective of a nation is to maximize the standard of living of all citizens.
- It is a fundamental economic law that the only sustainable way to continuously increase the standard of living is to increase productivity, therefore productivity growth must be maximized while maintaining demand/supply equilibrium in goods, services, labor and money supply.
- Policies are enacted to maximize productivity growth. Productivity gains determine the *"supply expansion capacity"* of the nation.

Productivity Economics

- International trade equilibrium (*mandated balanced trade*) is managed and controlled by international trade agreement or import tax policy. This ring-fences economies so their economies can be regulated independently at a national level.

- International trade is encouraged to achieve *comparative advantage* productivity gains.

- Base rate (minimum) wages and working hours are adjusted according to the combined productivity gains and inflation targets so that the national base rate wage goes up by the national productivity gain plus the target inflation rate. This determines the *"demand expansion capacity"* of the nation and is regulated to match the *supply expansion capacity* to maintain full employment and to maintain supply/demand equilibrium.

- Excess inflation/supply shortages caused by economic shocks (such as the 1973 oil crisis) are managed through supply stimulation and demand suppression using money supply, higher interest rates or other savings incentives.

- Deflation/ Demand shortages caused by economic shocks such as the Great Financial Crisis (GFC) are managed through demand stimulation such as government spending, base (minimum) wage increases, money supply expansion, private spending incentives (interest rates or other spending incentives) and supply suppression.

Making Capitalism Work Again

Productivity Equilibrium Economics doesn't replace Keynesian or monetarism economics; it is a top layer.

20. Solution 2: Change the Federal Reserve Mandate

The USA Federal Reserve (central bank) already has a dual mandate to control both inflation and employment, but it has limited tools available to achieve it. Primarily these tools are the money supply and control of interest rates.

The implementation of a *balanced trade mandate* changes everything.

It enables the Federal Reserve to utilize *Productivity Equilibrium Economics* to more effectively regulate the economy and employment.

Excess inflation can be effectively controlled by setting interest rates. The Federal Reserve has a long and successful history of doing this. Increasing interest rates applies the brakes to the economy.

Deflation cannot be prevented using interest rates or money supply. Taking your foot off the brake does not cause the car to accelerate.

The Federal Reserve rules should be changed so that the minimum allowable Federal Reserve rate (the Fed rate) is the rate of inflation plus the marginal income tax rate on interest income at the median income level.

> 2014 Median Income = $28,800 [21]
>
> 2014 Federal tax rate on median income = 15 percent

In 2014 the minimum interest rate would be around 1.6 percent plus 15 percent = 1.84 percent.

This rate is the minimum rate that provides wealth preservation for middle-class savers. Anything less destroys the wealth of savers. Negative real interest rates are a government endorsed and sponsored transfer of wealth from the middle class to the rich. It is an act of economic desperation and it is coming close to meeting Albert Einstein's definition of insanity.

In November 2015 the US Fed rate was 0.25 percent, and it was increased to 0.5 percent in December 2015.[22]

Allowing the Federal Reserve to set the minimum wage provides a new tool that allows excessively low inflation or deflation to be managed, as well as a means to couple wages to productivity growth.

If the country is experiencing deflation or excessively low inflation after interest rates have been reduced to the minimum allowable level, the Fed would increase the minimum wage. This will immediately cause an increase in demand, inflation, and GDP as shown in the previous chapters. This is counter-intuitive, because in the past the opposite happened, but "*mandated balanced trade*" changes everything.

Before, if the minimum wage was increased, companies would move their production to lower-cost offshore locations. With "mandated balanced trade" this is not viable because tariffs will increase by more than the savings.

Productivity Economics

Interest rates are the brakes. The national minimum wage level is the accelerator. The rate of inflation and employment can be regulated much more directly and precisely.

In a *mandated balanced trade regime,* raising the minimum wage faster than productivity gains increases consumption and inflation. It increases inflation because vendors incur increased labor costs that must be passed on to the consumer.

It increases demand because low-income people spend all their income. If you pay them more money, they will spend it. It is like a direct cash injection into the economy. During times of excessively low demand and inflation the benefits of increasing demand are greater than the costs of increasing wages.

Increasing the minimum wage increases consumption, inflation, and GDP. The wage increase will trickle up to the middle class, increasing their disposable income and hence further increasing demand. Disposable income will go up for the majority of people. Demand for goods and services will increase.

The present economy is demand constrained. One of the biggest problems that companies face, particularly domestic companies, is that demand is stagnant. Supply and demand are unbalanced and there needs to be considerable demand stimulation. Increasing the minimum wage solves this. The poor will be able to afford more hamburgers, TVs, cars and smart phones, and that will trickle up to everybody. Trickle up, not trickle down. It will lead to a return to nominal growth and inflation. It will create a virtuous circle, but only if there is *mandated balanced trade.*

The Federal Reserve will have the tools to effectively regulate the economy during times of both high inflation and low inflation.

Figure 20-1 Table of Key Economic Metrics

Metric (annual change)	Status Quo	Productivity Equilibrium Model
Inflation	2%	2%
Productivity Growth	1.3% *	2 to 3%
GDP Growth	2%	4%
Minimum Wage Increases	0%	3 to 4%
Fed Interest Rate	0.5%	3%
Bank Term Deposit (3 yr)	1.6%	4%
Mortgage Rate (30 yr)	3.5%	5%

* the actual productivity growth of US companies is higher but much of the gain is being realized offshore.

Figure 20-1 shows an estimate of how various economic metrics would be affected by the Productivity Equilibrium Model. The biggest impact is that GDP growth would be much higher, interest rates would return to normal levels that provide real returns to savers, and wages would increase by 3 to 4 percent annually. Mortgage rates would increase however the effects of annual pay increases more than offset the increase because the mortgage is a fixed cost. A home owner is far better off over time with higher mortgage rates and steadily increasing wages than with very low mortgage rates and stagnant wages. Note that inflation does not increase if the minimum wage increases equal productivity increases.

21. Coupling Wages to Productivity

The best way to couple wages to productivity is to control the national minimum wage. You do not need to control all wages. If you control the minimum wage in a balanced economy where companies compete for workers, you will effectively control all wages because people will be paid in accordance with their marginal contribution over an unskilled worker. The key is to maintain full employment so that labor demand slightly exceeds supply, unless inflation is too high.

Productivity coupling changes the way corporations think. Before, if you increased productivity then expenses would go down and profits would go up. Long term, this causes declines in demand, employment, wages and standards of living. With *productivity coupling*, if you increase productivity then revenue will increase, expenses will stay the same or increase slightly, and profits will increase. Long term this causes increases in demand, employment, and wages and standards of living.

The productivity-driven wage increase will affect all companies. Their wage costs will increase in proportion to the national productivity increase regardless of whether individual companies have been able to increase productivity. Relative labor costs will decrease for companies whose productivity increased by more than the average. Relative labor costs will increase for companies whose productivity increase was below average. Increasing wage costs and the need to remain competitive will drive companies to maximize productivity improvements. Demand will increase in proportion to the wage increase for most companies.

Productivity Economics

Companies that cannot pass on their increased costs will fail. The market will work as it should and the best companies will thrive and the worst will falter. It will be true productivity-driven creative destruction working as it should.

This raises the philosophical question of why the benefits of productivity improvements should be distributed to minimum wage workers, rather than to the capitalists who provided the capital that implemented the productivity improvement, or the knowledge worker who provided the expertise that enabled the productivity improvement. There are several answers.

First, it was probably the minimum wage worker whose productivity was improved. They are the ones producing more. Most automation is targeted at simple repetitive tasks that are relatively easy to automate. Examples are airline check-in, retail store checkout, and simple manufacturing tasks.

Second, it is a "Social Dilemma" situation, where everybody in the value chain benefits from the productivity increase if the minimum wage increases, and only a few benefit if it does not. By increasing the minimum wage in proportion to the productivity improvement, there will be trickle up wage increases for everybody, including knowledge workers and managers. There will never be a situation where a skilled worker earns less than an unskilled worker, unless some other factor like danger plays a role.

Making Capitalism Work Again

Third, once it is recognized that productivity improvements are universally beneficial and that companies must increase productivity to compete, it will accelerate the pace of automation. Skilled workers who can enable automation will be more highly valued.

Fourth, the only way investors can earn a return on investment in productivity improvements in the long run is if demand increases. The economy only works if supply and demand are in equilibrium. If productivity is improved and demand (sales) increase by more than the productivity improvement, then the investment will earn a good return. Henry Ford understood that in order for his idea of mass production to work and be profitable, his workers needed to be able to afford his products. Henry Ford was one of the great pioneers who started the trend that led to America becoming the wealthiest nation on earth. He didn't pay his workers the least he could; he paid them in accordance with their productivity and he did everything he could to enhance that productivity.

And finally, productivity improvements are largely made possible by the infrastructure of the nation. They are the result of the system of government, the education system, the national knowledge base, the intellectual property laws, the transportation, power, communications systems, infrastructure etc. that facilitate the development of new ideas and technologies. This enabling infrastructure is all part of the commons and the benefits should be distributed accordingly.

22.   Solution 3: Change Corporate Taxation

There are several ways to level the playing field for US domestic companies. The simplest way would be to just reduce US corporate income tax rates to around 20 percent so that they are internationally competitive, however there are many downsides to that approach.

A much better way is to replace the US corporate income tax with a national corporate goods and services tax (GST).

The GST is generally viewed as a regressive consumption tax paid by the consumer, but there is another way to look at it. If the GST is viewed as a corporate tax, you get a very different perspective.

The corporate income tax is exactly as regressive as a GST. The effect of corporate income tax on the end price of a product is exactly the same in dollars for the poor as for the rich. It is a regressive tax, not a progressive tax where the rich pay more.

The reality is that the customer pays for everything, including corporate income taxes. The price of a product or service includes the materials, labor, cost of sales, taxes including income tax, and profit. The end price (including all taxes) of a good is defined by the law of supply and demand.

If a company can produce goods or a service, pay all overheads and taxes and make a profit, then the product and company are viable. It does not make a difference to the end customer or the selling price if the tax component is a 35 percent tax on profits, or an equivalent GST, but it does make a big difference to the overall economy and where that product is made.

The proposed federal GST is a corporate tax. It should be included in prices and be invisible to the end customer, just as corporate income tax is.

Instead of taxing companies for the privilege of residing in a country, which companies care less and less about, as evidenced by the increasing number of reverse mergers, you tax access to the market, which companies care about very much. Companies are mobile and they can easily move their nominal base and profit centers to the country of least resistance, but markets are fixed and companies cannot move them or exist without them. Taxes on access to the market are something that corporations cannot avoid, and they pay it regardless of where they reside.

There is another distortion caused by corporate income taxes. Profitable companies pay high tax and unprofitable companies pay no tax and get a free ride. They both rely on and use the physical and social infrastructure, legal systems and protection of the nation. Profitable companies are subsidizing unprofitable companies and companies who arrange not to earn much profit like Amazon, and companies who arrange to earn most of their profits on products that they sell in the USA in overseas subsidiaries. These distortions are counterproductive to productivity growth and GDP growth. A corporate GST based on sales fixes this problem.

Productivity Economics

Replacing the federal corporate income tax with a corporate GST will have a significant positive impact on wealth creation, effective taxation rates of offshore companies, the economics of offshore manufacturing, and government revenues.

With the present regime of taxes on corporate profits, US corporations pay on average much more US income tax on products sold in the USA than do corporations or subsidiaries that are domiciled outside the USA.

Minimal US income taxes are paid on most imported products. The profits are all recorded in low tax jurisdictions. It is legal, so companies are compelled to do it to remain competitive.

The GST is a value added tax (VAT) applied to all goods and services sold. Vendors collect the tax as part of each sale. Vendors pay the government the difference between the GST that they collect when they sell the product minus the GST they paid on their inputs such as raw materials, sub-assemblies or services provided by others as an input. Thus the GST is paid on the value added at each stage of the supply chain. There is no offsetting GST input deduction for imports, so imports incur the GST at the landed price plus the GST on local value added by local processing, local transport and the retailer etc.

GST would not be paid on any product or service that is exported.

Many countries including Canada, Australia, and all of Europe have implemented GST or VAT taxes. The USA is the only G20 country that does not have a GST or VAT. US companies pay GST in all countries that they export to. Foreign companies do not pay GST when they sell in the USA.

Some countries that have a GST such as Canada, the UK, Ireland, and the Netherlands have used their GST revenues to reduce corporate income taxes. This has given them a competitive advantage versus the USA, and it encourages US companies to locate their corporate headquarters in these countries.

The mechanisms for implementing and collecting GST are well understood and proven, and they are much more efficient and effective than collecting corporate income tax.

The USA has one big advantage in that it does not have a national GST. Can you imagine the competitive advantage US based companies would have if corporate income taxes were replaced by a GST? There would be zero net cost change for companies producing and selling in the US, but costs for offshore suppliers would go up by the amount of the GST. The cost of foreign sales for US-made products and services would go down because they would no longer pay US income tax or US GST on foreign sales. This alone might be sufficient to solve the US trade deficit problem.

GST in lieu of corporate income taxes also has the advantage that government revenues would be much less volatile. During recessions corporate profits and income taxes can fall by 50 or more percent, but GDP may only fall by 2 or 3 percent. In recessions government income from corporate income taxes plunge, but GST taxes will only decline by a few percentage points. The plunging government revenue makes it much more difficult for governments to properly apply Keynesian stimulus during recessions.

The GST is a much more efficient tax. Corporate income taxes are very complex to administer and enforce. They require an army of government accountants, lawyers, auditors etc. to administer. The US corporate income tax includes tax on offshore profits, so the IRS sends expensive professionals overseas to audit offshore branches of US companies. Large US corporations also have armies of accountants and lawyers to administer and optimize corporate income taxes. By comparison, GST taxes are local, very simple, efficient and much more difficult for corporations to avoid. I may have just gifted the USA a 1 percent productivity improvement.

Replacing income tax with GST will have a significant beneficial effect on small businesses. They would no longer need to devote administrative and capital resources to calculating and paying income taxes. Income tax arrears cause a significant number of small business bankruptcies, and it is often because these small companies do not have the expertise to do proper tax planning, to properly document and account for tax obligations, or to accrue tax reserves. GST administration is simple, it is pay as you go, and it is much less likely that small companies will get in trouble.

Lower tax rates in themselves will not cause US companies to hire more people. Only increased demand for products made in the USA will do that. In order for the proposed balanced trade mandate to work, the corporate tax playing field must be leveled so that there is not a disincentive to produce in the USA.

Depending on how it is implemented, GST can either be revenue neutral or it can generate new revenue for the federal government.

The GST is an important part of solving the trade balance problem.

23. Balanced Trade Analysis

Figure 23-1 Trade Statistics by Country

WTO 2014 Trade Data	GDP	Exports Goods& Services	Imports Goods& Services	Trade Balance	Trade Balance	Import Duties
Country	$ bill	$ bill	$ bill	$ bill	%	%
USA	17,419	2309	2865	-556	-3.2%	3.5%
Japan	4,601	842	1012	-170	-3.7%	4.2%
India	2,049	478	610	-132	-6.5%	13.5%
France	2,829	850	926	-76	-2.7%	5.3%
Brazil	2,346	264	325	-61	-2.6%	13.5%
Turkey	798	208	265	-58	-7.2%	10.7%
UK	2,989	843	881	-38	-1.3%	5.3%
Mexico	1,295	419	444	-25	-1.9%	7.5%
Canada	1,785	560	581	-21	-1.2%	4.2%
Indonesia	889	199	211	-12	-1.3%	6.9%
Australia	1,455	294	299	-5	-0.3%	2.7%
Spain	1,404	459	428	30	2.2%	5.3%
Korea	1,410	679	640	39	2.8%	13.3%
Switzerland	701	424	369	55	7.9%	6.7
Italy	2,141	645	585	60	2.8%	5.3%
Netherlands	879	859	744	116	13.1%	5.3%
Russia	1,861	563	427	136	7.3%	8.4%
Saudi Arabia	746	364	222	142	19.0%	11.1%
Germany	3,868	1774	1542	232	6.0%	5.3%
China	10,355	2574	2341	233	2.2%	9.6%
Total	61,821	15,604	15,716	(112)	-0.2%	

Source: World Trade Organization database.

Figure 23-1 shows world trade statistics for 2014.

Making Capitalism Work Again

The top twenty countries in terms of GDP are shown, listed in order of trade balance in dollars. They have a combined GDP of over $61 trillion and trade accounts for about a quarter of that. These countries represent about 85 percent of world GDP. Trade at the world level is close to being balanced.

The USA has the largest trade deficit, at $556 billion or 3.2 percent of GDP. China and Germany have the largest trade surplus. In percent terms, China's surplus is only 2.2 percent and they have high import duties, so it would not be very difficult for them to adjust to a *balanced trade mandate.*

The countries that would have the biggest problems would be Germany, Saudi Arabia, Switzerland, the Netherlands, and Russia. It is interesting to note that some of the countries with large trade surpluses also have very high import duties. These nations do not intend to trade; they want to maximize wealth accumulation. Some of these are resource countries, so it is understandable that they would want to accumulate wealth since their resource is being depleted. However, they are doing this at the expense of their trading partners and middle-class workers. Australia and Canada are also resource countries and their trade is close to being balanced.

The *balanced trade mandate* does not mean that countries cannot run a trade surplus. It just means that if they do, their markets must be totally open with zero duties and free access to their market. They can't have it both ways.

Productivity Economics

24. Implementing Balanced Trade

A two tier GST may be the most efficient way to implement a *balanced trade mandate*.

All domestically produced goods and services would be taxed at the domestic dGST rate, and imported goods and services taxed at the Import iGST rate. When trade is balanced or in surplus the two are the same, but when you have a trade deficit the Import iGST rate would be higher by the formula amount.

There are two ways the dGST rate could be set.

The dGST rate can be set so that the government proceeds exactly equal the proceeds from the present federal corporate income tax. This is revenue neutral for the government. This results in a tax deduction for domestic producers since GST on imports will provide a portion of the revenue. It is a tax increase for offshore producers.

Alternatively, the dGST can be set so that the government proceeds from US companies exactly equal the domestic income tax proceeds (excluding foreign income). This is tax neutral for US domestic producers but the dGST is a cost increase for offshore producers. The GST on imports generates new government revenue.

Total US business sales in 2014 were approximately $16 trillion. [23] The total federal government corporate income tax revenue was $417 billion, so, using the first method, an equivalent GST rate would be 2.6 percent.

A rate of 2.6 percent is remarkably low. It is probably not much more than the administrative cost companies incur for income taxes, not to mention the administrative cost associated with the IRS.

The iGST would be set to 3 times the trade deficit percentage.

The advantage of having a dGST and an iGST is that there is only one bureaucracy required to administer and enforce the system, as opposed to the present system where there are two or three vast government bureaucracies to deal with.   It generates another productivity improvement.

There is just one tax structure that applies uniformly to all goods and services and there is no corporate income tax. It is simple and efficient.

Using the 3 times formula, the iGST would be the dGST plus 9.6 percent (3.2% x 3). The iGST component would be phased in over a number of years, for example starting at 5 percent and increasing each year until the formula rate is reached. Of course it would never get to 9 percent. In fact, I believe that US trade would be nearly balanced within 3 years.

If the dGST was 3 percent, the initial USA impact of a G20 balanced trade policy implemented using the iGST would be an initial 8 percent increase (3% dGST + 5% iGST) in the cost of imported goods. This would cause an increase in prices of imported goods. This would be offset by increased competitiveness of domestic producers and new government iGST revenues so the government deficit would come down.

Productivity Economics

There would be zero impact on the cost of domestically produced goods since the dGST is exactly offset by the elimination of corporate income tax.

The biggest immediate impact of the balanced trade policy is that it makes it very risky for corporations to move production to lower-cost regimes. It they do so collectively, the iGST will go up and domestic producers will have a competitive advantage.

There would be a small decrease in US income taxes that offshore producers pay on US profits, but it would be small because companies endeavor to realize most of their profits offshore.

The price of imported energy will increase by the iGST amount, so domestic producers will experience increased demand and better margins.

If the policy is implemented simultaneously with a substantial minimum wage increase, demand and GDP will rise.

Over time, trade would move towards balance, causing:

- An accelerating shift to domestic energy sources such as oil, natural gas, bio-fuel, solar and wind.

- The manufacture of high value goods to be brought back to the USA, causing an increase in high value employment.

- The economy to move towards full employment. Labor shortages will develop in areas, causing wages to increase and the labor force to shift towards the highest value added jobs. The middle class will start to grow again.

- The economy to grow and the trade and government deficit to decrease.

- An increase in both exports and imports, but they will move towards balance.

- The rich to get richer.

- Low and middle income workers to get richer and at a faster rate.

Longer term, large corporations will migrate towards producing in the area where the major markets are, or, when the iGST premium has fallen to zero, managing their own trade so that it is balanced and it takes advantage of comparative advantage.

How would countries with a large trade surplus react to this? The first thought is that there would be a trade war, but this won't happen because the export market is critical to keeping their citizens employed. A trade war would be suicide for them.

You can only have a trade war if you are engaged in trade. Countries with large trade surpluses are not, they are engaged in providing products for debt. They have several options: importing more by reducing their tariffs and regulatory obstacles, or letting their currency rise, which will cause imports to rise and exports to fall, and reduce their inflation. They could further subsidize their exports to counteract the tariff, but that is just exporting their wealth, so it would have to be a very short-term policy.

The USA is unique in that it is the world's reserve currency. Every other country has one more economic control variable, namely their exchange rate. If there is a *balanced trade mandate* and the US increases the minimum wage, costs, and inflation, every other country must compensate to maintain the balance. They can either increase their wages or the value of their currency versus the US. It amounts to the same thing.

Presently some countries manage their currency exchange rates to achieve a competitive advantage. With *mandated balanced trade*, they will manage their currency to achieve balance.

The reality is that it is not really China who will decide what to do, it is Walmart, Amazon, Apple, Dell, HP, Costco, Sears, Samsung, Sony, Home Depot, Toyota, Ford, General Motors and the big oil refiners etc. They control trade between China, Japan, Korea and the USA and between the big oil producers and the USA.

If trade is brought into balance without causing a long-term contraction in US consumption, US GDP will increase by 3.2 percent or $550 billion (the amount of the trade deficit), which will increase employment by over 5 million jobs at $100,000 per job. The US would essentially go to full employment or even beyond full employment.

If US GDP increases by 3.2 percent, US tax revenue will increase by a similar amount. The US debt to GDP ratio will go down and the US federal government deficit will go down. There would be substantial additional improvements in the government deficit caused by reduced unemployment and social programs.

If the US moves towards balanced trade, foreign counties will not have the $500 billion of trade surplus funds that they must invest in US Treasuries to prevent their currency from appreciating. The US government will need to find a new source of funds to finance their annual deficits. Interest rates will rise. It will make sense to save again.

In a balanced trade/full employment regime, unions become irrelevant, at least for wage negotiations. The work force will automatically gravitate to the jobs with the highest value add, which will pay the most. Wage agreements negotiated by unions in a balanced trade/full employment situation create distortions that amount to subsidies, thus reducing the overall productivity and wealth of the nation.

25. Europe Balanced Trade

For Europe the *balanced trade mandate* would probably be applied on a total European Union basis. The European Union countries already have a dGST. The iGST tax rate would be computed based on the total European Union trade balance and the iGST would be applied to all goods entering the European Union. The European Union had a goods and services trade surplus of about 2.5 percent of GDP in 2013 so the iGST adder would be zero so the iGST would be the same as the dGST. [24]

Economic theory dictates that in order for a free trade area with a common currency to work, you must have full labor mobility. The USA meets this criterion and it works. Europe does not really have true worker mobility because there are language, trade qualification, family, and culture issues that significantly restrict labor mobility. I was in Greece in the summer of 2015 when the government imposed currency controls and I specifically asked people why they didn't move to an area of Europe where there were better opportunities. For most, it was not even a possibility for the reasons listed. Most didn't even have European bank accounts outside Greece to allow them to avoid the currency controls. The European common market risks collapse because the key criteria for a free trade area are not in reality met.

The European Union tries to impose uniform tax, business, banking and labor practices throughout all of the common market area in order to allow free trade with fair competition. This regulation results in a large bureaucracy that overrides local culture and preference. *Mandated balanced trade* within Europe would eliminate the need for the regulations and bureaucracy while still allowing totally open trade. If there is *mandated balanced trade* local rules or subsidies do not make any difference to competition fairness. With *mandated balanced trade* subsidies damage the exporting country not the importing country.

It is interesting to consider how things would work if the *"mandated balanced trade"* policy was applied on a country-by-country basis within Europe.

If *mandated balanced trade* was implemented in Europe much of the reason for the existence of the European common market would disappear, since the whole world would become a common market. There are still sound reasons for retaining the Euro as a common currency, and for retaining various common regulatory functions and for freedom of movement, but if true labor mobility cannot be achieved long term, the only options are going back to individual currencies or implementing *mandated balanced trade* within Europe.

If *mandated balanced trade* was in effect at the G20 level, there would be little reason for the United Kingdom to remain in the European common market.

26. The Triffin Dilemma Revisited

I do not know whether it is possible to implement a *balanced trade mandate* without establishing a new reserve currency or at least a world reserve bank. I do know that it is necessary to restore trade balance if the middle class is to be preserved.

I do not have the expertise to suggest how the reserve currency issue should be resolved. John Maynard Keynes suggested a Bancor international reserve currency and that idea has been backed by several prominent economists, including Zhou Xiaochuan from China.[25]

> John Maynard Keynes envisaged much of this back in the 1930s, and attempted to devise a long-term solution. In the 1940s, at the Bretton Woods Conference, Keynes alongside E.F. Schumacher tried to implement a global financial arrangement—the International Clearing Union—to minimize trade imbalances and the frictions that they can create. The International Clearing Union would be a global bank whose job would be the clearance of trade between nations. All international trade would be denominated in its own unit of account, the proposed Bancor. The Bancor was to have had a fixed exchange with sovereign national currencies, and would have been used as a unit of account to measure the trade balance between nations. Every good exported would add Bancor to a country's account with the International Clearing Union, while every good imported would subtract Bancor. To discourage imbalances, if a nation had a high trade surplus the ICU would

take a percentage of its Bancor balance and put it into the Clearing Union's reserve fund; this would encourage nations with surpluses to buy other nations' exports. Nations that imported more than they exported would have their currency depreciated against the Bancor, thus encouraging other nations to buy their products, and making imports more expensive. [26]

27. Minimum Wage Considerations

In 2014 there were approximately 3 million US workers being paid at or below the federal minimum wage of $7.25. [27]

Mandated balanced trade makes it feasible and desirable to increase the national minimum wage.

Increasing the minimum wage to a living wage dramatically reduces the social support burden on government. People earning a living wage pay taxes and contribute to society, as opposed to those with a subsistence income that collect food stamps, and government provided social and medical services. Over 45 million people in the USA were receiving food stamps in 2015, costing over $73 billion.[28]

You, as a taxpayer, have a choice of paying a *living wage* directly at the cash register, or getting your products cheaper but having to pay enough taxes to provide essential social services for the poor. The tax route costs you at least 30 percent more because in order to pay out one dollar governments must collect at least $1.30 from you to cover the administrative costs of distributing benefits. Governments are not very efficient. It is much more efficient to pay a living wage directly.

> This is sometimes known colloquially as "Okun's bucket," after economist Arthur Okun, who once likened redistribution to moving wealth from one person to another with a leaky bucket. You manage to move some from one place to another, but along the way you lose some from leaks.

Modern empirical techniques have allowed economists to get a better idea of how big the leaks are in the bucket. For example, a recent paper by Nathaniel Hendren looks at the US earned income tax credit, food stamps and housing vouchers. He finds that for every dollar redistributed from rich to poor with those programs, anywhere from 34 cents to 56 cents leaks out and is lost. [29]

Paying a *living wage* directly constitutes a 30 percent productivity improvement over engaging the government to do it on your behalf.

In addition, there are all the negative long-term social issues of having a large portion of society living in poverty and dependent on social security. That population is living in, and dependent on, a welfare state.

If you want smaller, more efficient government, increase the minimum wage to a living wage.

If you want economic growth, increase the minimum wage to a living wage over a number of years, after you have implemented *mandated balanced trade*.

If you want lower taxes, increase wages sufficiently for all able-bodied working adults to be self-sufficient rather than depending on handouts from the state.

In the USA, depending on where you live, the minimum *living* wage for a couple, both working, with two children is around $12 per hour ($25,000 per year). The present minimum wage is $7.25, which equates to $15,100 per year.[30]

Productivity Economics

Australia is an example of what happens when you have near full employment and a living minimum wage ($16 to $20 AU per hour, depending on age and occupation). This is sufficiently high that a couple, both working at the minimum wage, can live and raise a family, while also paying taxes. With a living minimum wage, couples can afford to own a house, a car, buy medical insurance, and occasionally dine out and take vacations. Over time they are able to slowly build equity in their homes. This creates a virtuous circle of rising consumption, employment and wealth, a good education system, low crime rates and a healthier society. Australia has little poverty among able-bodied, able minded adults, and it is a vibrant society with a very high overall standard of living and quality of life.

Australia can afford this because most of its economy is comprised of non-portable industries such as construction, professional services, mining, agriculture and tourism. In 2014 Australia had a modest trade surplus of under 1 percent of GDP.

The virtuous circle is still operating in Australia. They have not had a recession since the 1990s, and they are the only G20 country that avoided recession during the 2007/8 Great Financial Crisis.

Australia has one of the lowest government debt/GDP ratios of any G20 country, at around 40 percent, compared to 96 percent in the USA and 196 percent in Japan in 2012. [31]

If you want a safer society, increase the minimum wage. People who accumulate assets such as cars and homes have something to lose, so they are less inclined to risk those assets on crime, and they are more inclined to promote safe neighborhoods to help protect and promote their assets.

Having full employment and a high minimum wage without the option of off-shoring provides corporations with an incentive to increase levels of automation. That increases productivity and high-income jobs. If there is a coupling of productivity to wages, everyone's standard of living increases.

In a full employment/balanced trade regime, the only way to increase real incomes and GDP is to increase productivity. As long as there is full employment, this increases national wealth and benefits everyone.

The Federal Reserve mandate should be enhanced to allow it to use the tools of controlling interest rates, money supply, and the national minimum wage to control inflation, to maximize GDP and productivity growth, and to maintain full employment.

28. Federal Reserve Role Change Implementation

Consider the situation in December 2015. Interest rates are near zero and real interest rates are negative. The US Federal Reserve just raised interest rates moderately to try move towards normalization of interest rates and to control future inflation, while still encouraging economic growth, which is well below the target range of 4 percent.

Overall, the economy is not doing too badly. Inflation is below the target rate of 2 percent, there is modest growth in GDP of around 2 percent (well under the 4 percent target rate), and unemployment has fallen to around 5 percent. Things are not too bad, but what happens if the Fed tries to normalize interest rates?

It is very risky. Raising interest rates will increase the cost of finance and it will have a disproportionate downwards effect on the disposable incomes of the working poor and the middle class. Demand will fall, employment will fall, and the risk of deflation will increase. Raising US interest rates while the rest of the world isn't will cause the US dollar to appreciate, which will cause imports to increase and exports to decrease. This reduces employment and GDP. It is a catch 22 situation. The Federal Reserve does not have the tools for a graceful normalization.

Now what would happen if there was a *balanced trade mandate* and instead the Federal Reserve raised the minimum wage? The wages and disposable incomes of low-income people would increase. They will spend all that increase. Demand will go up (see the chapter on minimum wage analysis). GDP will grow. As shown in the Productivity Case Study, inflation will not increase unless wages are increased by more than the national productivity increase.

When demand increases it is safe for the Federal Reserve to raise interest rates, as long as they do it in a manner that does not significantly compromise the increase in the disposable income of the poor and middle class.

This sequence can be repeated until we get to nominal growth, inflation, and interest rates. With *mandated balanced trade* it will not be attractive for companies to move production offshore.

Now the airplane has a throttle and an elevator control. Maybe in the future we will add ailerons and a rudder. Then we will really be able to fly.

29. Minimum Wage Analysis

The assertion that increasing the minimum wage in a *mandated balanced trade* environment is an effective and beneficial way to prevent excessively low inflation or deflation is not obvious and will certainly be contentious, so let's examine the issue in more detail.

Let's start with a logic exercise. Suppose we take an extreme case and double the US minimum wage from $7.25 to a $14.50 living wage in one step. What is the impact for a service business such as a fast food restaurant that uses all minimum wage employees?

Their labor costs will increase by 100 percent. In a typical restaurant business, direct labor accounts for about 30 percent of the operating costs. To keep it simple, let's assume it is a business with annual sales of $1,000,000.

Figure 29-1 shows the impact of the wage increase on spending for wages, fixed costs such as the mortgage, buildings and equipment, and variable costs such as raw materials and taxes.

The variable costs will increase by an amount equal to the induced rate of inflation, which will be less than 5 percent.

So if we double wages, prices must increase by 35 percent to maintain the same profit margins.

Making Capitalism Work Again

Figure 29-1 Restaurant Minimum Wage Increase Example

Restaurant Example	Before $K	Before % of Sales	After $K	After % Sales
Wages	$300	30%	$600	44%
Fixed costs	$300	30%	$300	22%
Variable costs	$300	30%	$315	23%
Profits	$100	10%	$135	10%
Total Sales	1,000	100%	1,350	100%
Food Price Inflation Effect			35%	
Variable Cost Inflation			5%	
Profit Increase			35%	

The biggest sectors employing minimum wage workers are food services, retail, and cleaning services. For companies like Walmart the labor component is much less than 30 percent of sales, so the example chosen is extreme. Doubling the minimum wage at Walmart would increase prices by less than 5 percent.

If there is little impact on sales volumes, the employees and the business owner are better off. The business owner makes more profit.

So, the million-dollar question is: will there be an impact on sales volumes?

Among major occupational groups, the highest percentage of hourly paid workers earning at or below the federal minimum wage was in service occupations, at about 10 percent. Almost two-thirds of workers earning the minimum wage or less in 2014 were employed in service occupations, mostly in food preparation and serving-related jobs.

The industry with the highest percentage of workers earning hourly wages at or below the federal minimum wage was leisure and hospitality (18 percent). Over half of all workers paid at or below the federal minimum wage are employed in this industry, the vast majority in restaurants and other food services. For many of these workers, tips may supplement the hourly wages received. [32]

Let's analyze it from the customer's point of view.

For minimum wage customers, who constitute a significant portion of the clientele for fast food restaurants and discount retail, the price has gone down in real terms. Their wages increased by 100 percent and their disposable income increased even more. Fast food prices increased by 35 percent. Minimum wage workers could afford more than three times as much fast food. The poor will get richer.

Low-income earners spend all their money. In fact, they spend more than all of their money because their increased incomes will qualify them for increased credit. They will spend more. Demand from this segment of society will increase. Businesses servicing this segment will prosper.

For the rich, a price increase of a dollar or two for a meal will make no difference and their spending patterns won't change. Food, services and consumer merchandise spending constitutes such a small percent of their income that they won't care, so their spending in this category in dollar terms will go up by the induced inflation amount. The rich will be pleased that sales and absolute profits have gone up. The capital value of these companies will increase. That is the income stream of the rich. The rich will get richer.

For the middle class it is more complicated. The minimum wage increase will trickle up the economic ladder, so provided that demand does increase, their wages will increase over time by the composite inflation increase.

So what effect will doubling the minimum wage have on overall inflation?

In 2014 there were approximately 3 million workers being paid at or below the federal minimum wage of $7.25 out of a total work force of 76 million. [33]

Minimum wage workers are a relatively small part of the economy. If you double their wages, driving a 25 percent average price increase in the products and services they provide (this is an extreme worst case), assuming that no one else's wages change, you will increase inflation by 3/76 x 25 percent = 1 percent. Of course the assumption is not reasonable, since all wages will be pushed up. That is the intent. The increases will be a declining exponential increase asymptotic on the final rate of inflation. This is a recursive formula, but I estimate that doubling the minimum wage will result in about 3 percent inflation and GDP growth.

So given that, let's assume that the middle class gets a 3 percent trickle up raise so that they do not fall behind. The 2015 US median wage is about $1147 per week, or $59,600 annually, so that is a $1,788 annual increase, much of which will be disposable income. Inflation benefits the middle class because their fixed costs, primarily their mortgage, does not increase, so their spending power goes up faster than the rate of inflation.[34]

Of course this is just a back of the napkin calculation and it is full of holes, but it gives a high-level view of the issues.

The US Federal Reserve inflation objective is 2 percent, so you would not implement the change in a single step, but with productivity increases around 2 percent and minimum wage increases there is no reason that the 2 percent inflation and 4 percent GDP growth objective cannot be met.

Note that this chapter is really just is a more detailed examination of Case D and E in chapter 14.

30. Minimum Wage Studies

There have been numerous studies of the effects of increasing the minimum wage. The results are inconclusive, with many showing that it is beneficial and some that it is not.

None of the studies have been done assuming a *balanced trade mandate*, whereby the work done by low wage workers cannot be moved offshore when wages are increased.

> Now, you might argue that even if the current minimum wage seems low, raising it would cost jobs. But there's evidence on that question—lots and lots of evidence, because the minimum wage is one of the most studied issues in all of economics. US experience, it turns out, offers many 'natural experiments' here, in which one state raises its minimum wage while others do not. And while there are dissenters, as there always are, the great preponderance of the evidence from these natural experiments points to little if any negative effect of minimum wage increases on employment.[35]

> [A] wave of new economic research is disproving those arguments about job losses and youth employment. Previous studies tended not to control for regional economic trends that were already affecting employment levels, such as a manufacturing-dependent state that was shedding jobs. The new research looks at micro-level employment patterns for a more accurate employment picture. The studies find minimum wage increases even provide

an economic boost, albeit a small one, as strapped workers immediately spend their raises.[36]

31. Minimum Wage Real World Results

A number of cities and states in the US, including Seattle and California, have implemented significant increases in the minimum wage. Again, the results are ambiguous as to whether this is beneficial or not. The fact that the results are ambiguous means that it has not done obvious or significant harm. These changes were made on a regional basis, where there is significant opportunity for economic leakage to lower-cost jurisdictions.

If significant minimum wage increases can be implemented without significant harm in jurisdictions where economic leakage is probable, then arguably they would be strongly beneficial in environments where the minimum wage increase is implemented on a national basis and there is a *balanced trade mandate* in place.

Another test of the validity of these conclusions is to look at world prices of Big Mac hamburgers in jurisdictions with different minimum wage levels. You can see that the wage impact on prices is much less than in the example. The example is worst case.

Figure 31-1 below shows the minimum wage by country in US dollars.

Figure 31-2 below illustrates that the countries with the highest minimum wage have the least expensive Big Macs in terms of the hours a minimum wage worker needs to work to buy a Big Mac.

Figure 31-1 Table of Minimum Wage by Country

Source: OECD Stats [37]

Figure 31-2 Hours of Work it Takes to Buy a Big Mac by Country

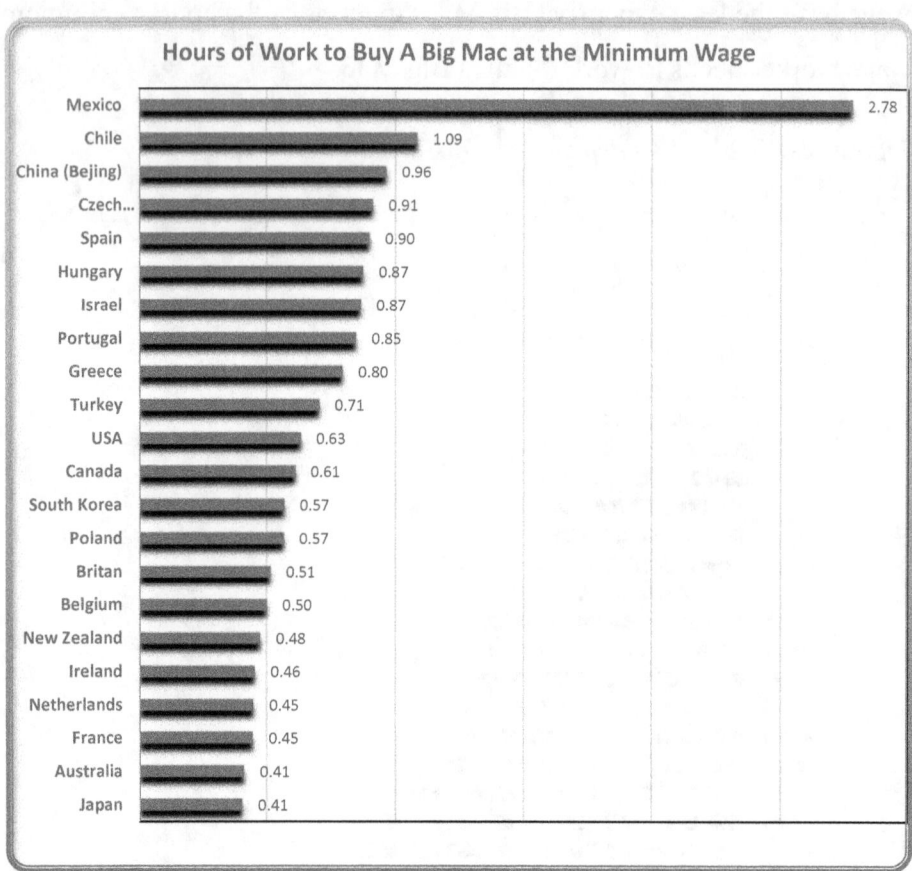

Source: *Global Price Info* [38]

The relative price of a Big Mac is lower in countries with a higher minimum wage. The price increase incurred by raising the minimum wage is less than the wage increase, so the relative cost goes down and demand from minimum wage workers increases.

32. Artificial Intelligence and Robots

One of the core tenants of capitalism is that companies and people compete and that the best will survive and thrive based on their merit. It is more complicated than that.

How well you do primarily depends upon your relative ability, the demand for the skills that you offer, and the number of people you compete against. If you are in the top skill decile in a field where there is healthy demand and limited supply of qualified people, you will do well. Top tradesmen, athletes, CEOs, financial people, lawyers, and doctors all do well.

For unskilled workers, everything is working against them. The demand for their services is declining because productivity improvements, stagnant domestic demand and global trade has made the labor pool essentially infinite, so wages are falling. Actually, US demand for the products and services provided by unskilled labor is increasing, but much of the work is going to the emerging markets.

With the introduction of Artificial Intelligence, even knowledge workers such as engineers, doctors, accountants and lawyers may start to see decreasing demand because of increasing productivity from AI. The income decline will start to penetrate above the median wage unless there is *mandated balanced trade* and *productivity coupling*. Merit will be insufficient to insure prosperity higher and higher up the value chain.

Productivity Economics

Maintaining full employment when there are continuous productivity improvements is a major issue. There is much discussion in the press about how the pending robot, additive manufacturing (3D printing), AI revolution, and driverless taxis, delivery vans and trucks is going to put everybody out of work.

> "It's not easy to estimate just how many human jobs will be replaced by robots. A 2014 Gartner presentation indicated that one in three jobs will be taken by smart machines by 2025. According to a lengthy 2013 Oxford paper, around 47 percent of total US employment is at high risk of automation over the next decade or two. Two high-tech industry pundits writing in *HBR* recently forecasted that nearly 30 percent of today's workforce will be of no economic value by 2025. Forrester's less extreme projection is that "16 percent of jobs will disappear due to automation technologies between now and 2025, but … jobs equivalent to 9 percent of today's jobs will be created." [39]

This trend is being called the "Fourth Industrial Revolution." "In the future, technological innovation will also lead to a supply-side miracle, with long-term gains in efficiency and productivity."[40]

Perhaps in the very long term the Fourth Industrial Revolution is a serious employment issue, but in the medium term until the "singularity" (the point where computers are more intelligent than humans) is reached, it does not need to be a problem. Artificial intelligence and robotics are just another form of productivity improvement.

Making Capitalism Work Again

Over the past five years there have been high levels of automation introduced in many functions, such as airline check-in, retail store checkout, warehouse operations etc. In spite of this there have only been annual productivity gains in the order of 1.3 percent. US productivity gains have probably been higher but some of the increase has been exported to other countries because of unbalanced trade. If we incentivized investments that improve productivity, as we should if we want to maximize the standard of living, we might get back to more normal levels of around 2 or 3 percent productivity growth. It is very hard for an advanced economy to achieve annual productivity improvements over 3 percent, and AI and robotics are unlikely to be any different.

In a properly regulated economy, with *productivity coupling* productivity improvements of 2 or 3 percent annually will result in steadily increasing real incomes, reduced workweeks, and optimal inflation. Thirty percent of jobs being automated over 10 years is less than 2.7 percent annually. During the Golden Age of Capitalism productivity growth averaged 2.8 percent so 2.7 percent is perfectly manageable and desirable. Managed correctly it is a great outcome where everybody's standard of living increases by 30 percent over ten years. It is not something to fear.

Alternatively, if it is not managed correctly and laissez-faire economics is allowed to run its course, the benefits of the productivity improvements will only go to the owners of the machines. This would result in falling standards of living for all wage earners. It could rupture society.

Productivity Economics

The key is that if the benefits of productivity improvements are coupled back into the economy properly, then demand increases, profits increase, employment increases, and real take-home wages and living standards increase substantially over time, while inflation is still kept in control. The faster productivity increases the higher the real growth in standard of living. Bring on the robots.

Once artificial intelligence moves beyond the "singularity," the future for humans is unknowable, especially if we allow corporations or a small number of individuals to own the AI.

33. Inflation Control

When you think about it, using interest rates to control inflation is a rather crude tool. Increasing interest rates makes credit more expensive and it encourages savings, both of which reduce demand and inflation. Money saved or money not borrowed is money that is not spent. It works.

However, when all you have is a hammer, everything looks like a nail. Sometimes a scalpel might be better.

Increasing capital investment in production capacity or productivity improvements also reduces inflation by increasing supply or reducing costs. The recent massive productivity improvements that have enabled shale oil production in the USA and the resulting price decline of oil is a good illustration.

The problem with increasing interest rates is that it also reduces capital investment, thus reducing supply and reducing productivity growth. This is counterproductive.

Raising interest rates is putting on the brakes. That is why we often go into recession when the Federal Reserve starts tightening. When your economy is going a bit too fast you don't really need to hit the brakes, you just need to ease your foot off the accelerator. Raising interest rates does reduce demand, but it also reduces future supply, which is exactly the wrong thing to do.

A better way to control inflation is to stimulate saving, which reduces demand, and to stimulate investment in production capacity or productivity improvements, which increases supply. This incentivizes beneficial behavior rather than discouraging detrimental behavior. A scalpel rather than a hammer. A carrot rather than a stick.

Many countries have tax free saving or investment plans to promote retirement savings, but they are not moderated in accordance with the supply/demand balance of the economy.

These tools will allow much higher rates of sustained growth in GDP and living standards without excess inflation.

We have also seen that limiting minimum wage increases to just the productivity growth also reduces demand, so this would be another tool available to the Federal Reserve.

Historically when the minimum wage was being increased regularly the increases were tied to the cost of living index. Again this is the wrong thing to do because it provides positive feedback to inflation and it amplifies the magnitude of the economic cycle. The correct thing to do is to increase wages by the productivity gain plus around 2 percent when inflation and growth are low, and by just the productivity gain when inflation is high. This provides negative inflation feedback and it dampens the magnitude of the economic cycle. Over the course of the economic cycle wages will still track the cost of living but economic stability will be improved.

The same argument applies to indexed pensions and other social benefits. Increases should be linked to productivity, not the cost of living. Any further adjustments to account for the cost of living should be out of sync with the economic cycle to dampen rather than reinforce the magnitude of the cycle.

There were some wild swings in inflation levels during the 1950's, 1960's and 1970's that were partially driven by the positive feedback provided by cost of living linked labor contracts etc.

From the end of WWII until 1970 demand grew rapidly and the principle problem was inflation. Stimulating supply growth to match demand solves the problem. This worked from 1945 until 1970 because a supply-side virtuous circle was in effect. The 1929 depression, the 1990 Japanese recession and the lingering 2008 GFC are instances of demand-side collapse. The central bank needs effective tools to manage both supply-side and demand-side economic factors.

Franklin Roosevelt implemented the "New Deal" demand-side stimulation to help end the Great Depression, then the Second World War finished the job. War is the ultimate demand-side stimulation. This time let's try something less drastic.

34. The Limits of Growth

Constantly increasing productivity growth and demand has the potential to strain the limited capacity of the earth and the environment.

At its essence, productivity growth is about doing more with less. It is not inherently detrimental to the environment or earth's resources. This is reflected by the declining energy and carbon dioxide intensity of developed countries. For example, we drive cars that have more features and perform better, yet they are more fuel efficient and much cleaner than older cars.

As productivity increases, society will have a choice between consuming more while working the same hours, or working less to maintain the same lifestyle and consumption levels. Both improve the standard of living. It is a choice for society to make. Most of the growth in the economy will be in the service sector. The service sector uses fewer resources per capita and per dollar of GDP than manufacturing.

35. The Fork In The Road of Capitalism

Capitalism has come to a fork in the road.

The wealth and income gap between the rich and the rest has primarily been caused by the breakdown of *income participation* where there is a link between productivity growth and income growth. *Income participation* is not new. *Income participation* is what made the Golden Age of Capitalism work so well. *Income participation* allowed all income groups to participate in the growing wealth of the nation. The *productivity coupling* that provided *income participation* has broken down and now nearly all the benefits are going to the rich. What is new in this book is the concept of using the Federal Reserve to regulate *productivity coupling* in order to recreate *income participation* and to regulate the economy to achieve growth and inflation objectives and to ensure that all society participates in the growing wealth of the nation.

If you do not have "income participation," then you must have "income redistribution" or you will have political extremism or anarchy.

The resolution, or not, of this economic problem has important political implications. It will define the shape of Western democracy in the future.

The key issue is how government convinces the young and those who end up in the bottom portion of the social economic strata that the system is fair, that their future prospects are good, and then delivers on that promise.

Logically there are only two social economic models that are likely to evolve in the USA and the Western World.   There are two basic

113

propositions that politicians can put to the people. We are at a fork in the road and voters will choose which way to go.

One choice is a social democracy with *income redistribution* probably in the form of a *basic income* for everybody.

The term social democracy has widely varying definitions, but for the purposes of this book, I will use the Wikipedia definition:

> Social democracy is a political ideology that supports economic and social interventions to promote social justice within the framework of a capitalist economy, and a policy regime involving welfare-state provisions, collective bargaining arrangements, regulation of the economy in the general interest, redistribution of income and wealth, and a commitment to representative democracy. Social democracy thus aims to create the conditions for capitalism to lead to greater egalitarian, democratic and solidaristic outcomes, and is often associated with the set of socioeconomic policies that became prominent in Western and Northern Europe – particularly the Nordic model in the Nordic countries – during the latter half of the 20th century.[41]

Finland is leading the way by proposing an unconditional national *basic income* for all regardless of economic contribution. There are many countries considering implementing a *basic income* policy. Google "basic income" to see how pervasive this idea has become.[42]

Making Capitalism Work Again

2016 Presidential candidate Bernie Saunders has declared that he favors a social democracy along the lines of the Nordic model and he has stated that he is "sympathetic" to the idea of *basic income*. He is receiving considerable attention and support, particularly among the young. Bernie Saunders is a wakeup call. [43]

The alternative is a liberal democracy with *"income participation,"* where all workers participate in the growing wealth of the nation by working and contributing and having their wages coupled to productivity growth.

There are also many definitions of liberal democracy. Liberal democracy is generally associated with more conservative or right wing individualistic viewpoints.

> Over time, the meaning of the word "liberalism" began to diverge in different parts of the world. According to the *Encyclopedia Britannica*, "In the United States, liberalism is associated with the welfare-state policies of the New Deal program of the Democratic administration of Pres. Franklin D. Roosevelt, whereas in Europe it is more commonly associated with a commitment to limited government and laissez-faire economic policies." Consequently, in the US, the ideas of individualism and laissez-faire economics previously associated with classical liberalism became the basis for the emerging school of libertarian thought. [44]

> Broadly speaking, liberalism emphasizes individual rights. It seeks a society characterized by freedom of thought for individuals, limitations on power, especially of government and

religion, the rule of law, the free exchange of ideas, a market economy that supports relatively free private enterprise, and a transparent system of government in which the rights of all citizens are protected. In modern society, liberals favor a liberal democracy with open and fair elections, where all citizens have equal rights by law and an equal opportunity to succeed. [45]

By these definitions, the governments of Western Europe, Canada, and Australia are all becoming social democracies. The US Democrats are straddling the fence and the US Republican Party advocates a liberal democracy, but they do not deliver on its core provisions.

The US Republican version of liberal democracy includes the provision that "[i]t is the government's role to enable people ... to secure the benefits of society for themselves ... government should only intervene when society cannot function at the level of the individual." [46]

Society clearly is not functioning at the level of the individual if able-bodied adults are not able to earn a fair living income. The problem is that the world has changed and no government has been successful at fulfilling this commitment in modern times.

36. When You Come to a Fork in the Road, Take It

— (Yogi Berra)

I believe that a fully functioning liberal democracy can be built on the principle that *it is the obligation of the state to ensure available employment with a living wage for all able-bodied adult citizens, and that they in turn are expected to be self-sufficient and contribute more to society than they take out over the course of their lifetime.*

Given either a right to income security under a social democracy, or a right to opportunity under a liberal democracy, I believe that voters will choose the latter, particularly in the United States where there is a strong bias towards independence and individual freedom. If people believe that the government can meet the commitment to *ensure the benefits of society for most people*, Americans would prefer to be self-sufficient rather than relying on the state for their financial wellbeing.

Social democracy requires a large bureaucracy. Collecting and redistributing wealth is a highly authoritarian and administrative process, and whether you are rich or poor, young or old, bureaucrats will have significant influence and control over your life. This is abhorrent to most people. People value freedom above most things. Redistributing wealth may work in times of abundance but redistribution is less likely to work in times of scarcity.

Productivity Economics

The liberal democracy model is much more autonomous. Government sets the rules but individual citizens interact freely among themselves, acting in their own self-interest, but constrained by rules that encourage them to behave in a manner that is also beneficial to society and the nation as a whole. In a properly structured system the bureaucracy and the individual's interaction with government is minimal.

I believe many people are aware of the limitations and problems of social democracies, and that the liberal democracy model is inherently more appealing to most people than the social democracy model. People want to be self-sufficient, independent and to contribute.

The liberal (conservative) political organizations in the Western World believe that the social democracy path we are on, with its large social programs and deficits, leads to failure and a loss of freedoms, but they are unable to articulate an alternative program that resonates with the majority of voters. The concept that if you have laissez-faire capitalism and reduce taxes the benefits will trickle down to everybody is tired and worn, and, as I have demonstrated it is not true. This story is no longer marketable to the majority.

Consider the following excerpt from an article in *The Atlantic* by T. Stanley and A. Lee:

> Twenty-five years ago this summer, Francis Fukuyama announced the "end of history" and the inevitable triumph of liberal capitalist democracy... But most disturbingly, the connection between capitalism, democracy, and liberalism upon

which Fukuyama's argument depended has itself been broken. In the wake of the credit crunch and the global economic downturn, it has become increasingly clear that prosperity is not, in fact, best served either by the pursuit of laissez-faire economics or by the inexorable extension of economic freedoms. Indeed, quite the opposite. As Thomas Piketty argues in *Capital in the Twenty-First Century*, free markets have not only enlarged the gap between rich and poor, but have also reduced average incomes across the developed and developing worlds. In the countries hardest hit by the recession—such as Greece and Hungary—voters have turned away from precisely that conception of liberalism that Fukuyama believed they would embrace with open arms. Across Europe, economic interventionism, nationalism, and even open racism have exerted a greater attraction for those casting their democratic votes than the causes of freedom, deregulation, and equality before the law. Liberal capitalist democracy hasn't triumphed. Instead, the failures of capitalism have turned democracy against liberalism. In turn, liberalism's intellectual self-identity has been left in tatters.

Sensing that Fukuyama's titanic argument has hit something of an iceberg, Liberal theorists have desperately been trying to keep the ship afloat. A raft of books have hit the shelves trying to breathe new life into liberalism, among which Larry Siedentop's *Inventing the Individual* and Edmund Fawcett's *Liberalism: The Life of an Idea* stand out. [47]

Productivity Economics

Or this quote from *Politico* concerning Donald Trump's popularity:

> That goes a long way to explaining the Trump phenomenon, which is plainly a reflection of public anger and a sense that something is terribly wrong with the country. The major economic indicators do not tell this story. The headline unemployment rate is now down to 5 percent, and last month showed signs that previously discouraged workers were re-entering the workforce. The Pew survey, however, shows that a significant minority of the country's population is slipping out of the middle class or barely maintaining its place. While the survey also shows a significant minority of the middle class is moving into the upper-income brackets, that hardly matters if you are the one slipping down.
>
> …
>
> Hence, no matter how decent "the economy" appears to be, many disaffected voters appear to feel that they are on the outside looking in. "Their economy" does not look like "the economy." Poll after poll indicates that the core of Trump's support comes from people with a high school degree or less, and for most people like this, the economy is not booming; it is not decent; it is collapsing and has been steadily deteriorating for decades. Wages overall are still stagnant, as they have been for years, and many jobs are lower paying, but costs are also flat or declining. [48]

Donald Trump and Bernie Saunders are a wake up call to the "one percent". Donald Trump is evidence that even conservative middle income voters are unwilling to accept the status quo. The appeal of Donald Trump and Bernie Saunders is that they are proposing to address the issue of falling low and middle income wages, and that they are outside of the political establishment that has failed these voters for so long. The solutions proposed by Trump and Saunders are not sufficient to solve the declining income problem but no one is proposing anything better.

37. The Fork in the Road: Left or Right

We have come to a fork in the road of capitalism.

One choice is to have a social democracy with a state funded national *basic income* regardless of economic contribution. This is the model that many Western democracies are moving to. The champions of the social democracy approach have a compelling story that is well articulated to the general population. Almost everyone in the lower economic half of society is likely to be better off in the short term with social democracy. Social democracy will *"enable people to secure the benefits of society for themselves"* in the short term.

A significant segment of society already has the belief that they do not need to pay taxes and that they are entitled to social benefits, income, and pensions from the state. They feel that the rich have an obligation to support them.

The other choice is a liberal democracy. One objective of this book is to define an even more compelling story for a liberal democracy that is more attractive to the electorate and more viable long term.

The key to that is to define an economic strategy that will deliver on the promise that *"it is the obligation of the state to ensure available employment with a living wage for all able-bodied adult citizens, and that they in turn are expected to be self-sufficient and contribute more to society than they take out over the course of their lifetime."*

Making Capitalism Work Again

The liberal democracy choice is only attractive to low-income voters if they are convinced that that commitment can and will be fulfilled and that their future will be better.

The key question is what social economic system best achieves this objective. Fundamentally, there are just two economic questions:

1. Which economic system creates the highest rate of wealth creation for a nation?
2. Which economic system is most effective at distributing that wealth among its citizens in a fair and equitable way?

The single most important metric for a functioning society is that the standard of living for low-income and middle-income people meaningfully increase over time.

The economic policy changes proposed in this book will provide government the tools to do a much better job of fulfilling that commitment and the commitment to employment with a living wage, and it will provide a means to allow all workers to participate in the economy. It will provide much faster economic growth than redistribution under a social democracy. Growth will be restored. Living standards will improve for everybody. The next generation will have a higher standard of living than the last at all income, skill and education levels.

The belief that the USA is the land of opportunity and that anyone can make it will become real again. Minimum wage workers will contribute and become taxpayers rather than a burden on the public purse.

Productivity Economics

It won't be foolproof. The economic cycle will still exist and there will be recessions, but growth of the middle class and faith in the future will be restored. Government will have better tools to manage the economic cycle and to compensate during the downturns.

The USA is the country that is the best positioned to lead the world in a different, more positive direction. The USA has one of the lowest federal government participation rates in the G20, and it has a strong tradition of independence, individuality, and self-reliance.

Figure 37-1 Social Democracy versus Liberal Democracy Table

Social Democracy	Liberal Democracy
Prioritize collective wellbeing	Prioritize individual wellbeing
Income redistribution. Unearned income	Income participation Earned income
Right to a basic income	Right to work for a living wage
Entitlement. Many people are wards of the state. They take more than they put in	People are independent. They put in more than they take out
Income limited by mean productivity	Income limited by personal productivity
Regulated capitalism	Responsible capitalism
Workers' rights protected by government or unions	Workers' rights protected by abundance of choice and competition for workers
Big government High government intervention in society and the individual's life	Small government Minimal government intervention
Heavy regulation (bureaucracy)	Heavy responsibility (tort law)
Robin Hood is a hero who takes from the rich and gives to the poor	Robin Hood is a villain who takes from those who have earned it and gives to those who haven't

38. Fulfilling the Living Wage Promise

The commitment that *"every able-bodied adult is entitled to employment at a living wage"* can be fulfilled by recreating the *productivity coupling* that made the Golden Age of Capitalism work. Productivity growth should be maximized, and the minimum wage should be directly linked to productivity growth under the control of the Federal Reserve.

In order for that to work trade must be balanced so that the benefits of national productivity growth are not exported.

In order to achieve maximum economic growth and full employment, the corporate tax regime must be changed so that domestic producers are not disadvantaged.

In order to achieve full employment, government must regulate the supply/demand curve for domestic labor. In order to do that, the supply/demand curve for domestic labor must be decoupled from the international labor market by implementing *mandated balanced trade,* then coupled to national productivity growth so that workers benefit from their growing productivity.

The Federal Reserve must be equipped with the tools to regulate the economy using the principles of the *"Productivity Equilibrium Economics Model."*

The best way to balance the growth of capital and the growth of worker incomes and upward mobility is to have a growing economy and permanent moderate worker shortages.

125

Productivity Economics

When trade is in balance and there is economic growth with full employment it will accelerate "creative destruction." Enterprises with higher productivity will be able to hire people away from low productivity companies. Higher productivity comes from deployment of capital. Each worker hired has a higher economic contribution, so he can be paid more.

Low productivity sectors will be forced to increase productivity to retain workers, which will create opportunities and growth in the technology sector and in higher value employment.

This pressure will stimulate investment and restore productivity growth to nominal levels

There will be upward mobility. The ranks of the middle class will rebuild.

The difference between now and the Golden Age for the middle class between 1945 and 1970 was that then there was a balance of power between capital and labor. As the economy grew the rich needed increasing amounts of labor to meet increasing demand and companies had to compete for that labor. Companies could only grow by increasing the demand for labor or increasing productivity, both of which drove the growth of the middle class.

39.   The Achilles Heel of Capitalism

The greatest strength of capitalism is its efficiency at using creative destruction to generate productivity improvements. No other economic system is so willing to destroy what it has created in favor of something better. However, as with many things, the greatest strength can be the greatest weakness.

In the Golden Age of Capitalism there was growing demand caused by favorable demographics and post WWII rebuilding. Capitalism is good at handling supply-side constraints. Increasing demand caused an increasing need for labor, creating a virtuous circle where the wealth of the middle class increased, causing demand to increase even more, increasing everyone's wealth. The virtuous circle repeated for many years. There was a power balance between capital and labor and the benefits of productivity improvements were shared.

Now, thanks to automation and an infinite world supply of cheap labor, the power balance between labor and capital is distorted. The Golden Age is over for Western countries. Now, when demand increases the incremental production either goes overseas or the levels of automation are increased. Companies no longer need domestic labor. The owners of capital still get richer because they operate at world level, and at a world level demand is still increasing. The owners of the means of production are still able to increase production at will and they make a profit on sales, but the virtuous circle is broken. The cycle no longer drives income growth for the low and middle income workers in Western countries.

Productivity Economics

Apple is a US company but if they sell a million more iPhones in China it is of little benefit to workers in the US or to the US government. Few incremental jobs are created in the US and the US government does not get much incremental tax revenue. The government does get deferred tax revenue on foreign profits that it may never be able to collect. The shareholders of Apple do benefit. The rich get richer.

Capital and the rich have the upper hand and capitalism is only working for a diminishing portion of the population. This is not sustainable in a democracy.

More productive companies will capture market share and become more valuable, but it is a zero sum game. An example is Amazon against the big retailers. The Amazon business model is a source of creative destruction that creates productivity improvements, but without *productivity coupling* it is just a zero sum force of disruption. There are winners and losers, but the GDP, government revenue and labor benefit value sum is zero, or even negative unless the productivity gains are coupled back into the economy to increase demand and worker participation.

Walmart is another example of a creative destruction business model that increased national productivity. Walmart led the import expansion. Walmart is the biggest importer from China and most of its employees are low-income workers. Walmart is another zero sum company because the economy was not structured to benefit from the productivity gains Walmart generated. To their credit they have just decided to increase their base wage to $10 per hour, and to increase all of their workers' wages. [49, 50]

Creative destruction is what America does best, but it needs to be done right so that it results in a growing economy and an increasing standard of living for all, otherwise it is just an unproductive force of disruption.

Companies need increasing demand. Domestic workers need increasing domestic demand. In the longer term, if demand doesn't increase there won't be capital growth, because without increasing demand there cannot be continuously increasing revenue and profits, and without increasing profits the capital value of companies cannot increase without increasing the price/earnings (P/E) multiples. Stock market price/earnings ratios are already at near historic highs and they are likely to fall if revenues and profits are not increasing.

Restoring economic health and growth requires:

- *mandated balanced trade* so that the benefits of comparative advantage are realized and so that production for incremental domestic demand stays in America.
- a *productivity coupling* mechanism, to ensure increasing productivity creates increasing wages and demand so that all society benefits.
- a balanced, fair international corporate tax system, so that domestic producers can compete fairly.

If productivity improvements are not fed back into the economy, the snake will eat its own tail.

40.   Productive and Zero Sum Capitalists

There are two types of capitalists. The first are "Zero Sum Capitalists," whose gain comes at someone else's expense.[51] It is win/lose. There is no net contribution to society. These are the capitalists represented by *The Big Short*, *The Wolf of Wall Street*, and hedge funds. They do not contribute to building economic capacity or productivity improvements. The Zero Sum Capitalists can make money in any economy, and many make the most money in times of economic stress. They don't create wealth, they just move it around and skim a percentage; often a large percentage. Capitalism is not supposed to be a zero sum game.

The other type are the "Productive Capitalists." They are the ones who invest and build companies, provide employment, and contribute to productivity growth. They are the capitalists that built America like Henry Ford, Thomas Edison, Bill Gates, Steve Jobs, Larry Ellison, John Rockefeller, Elon Musk, Thomas Watson Sr. (IBM), Warren Buffet, and Mark Zuckerberg, to name just a few. By building or financing companies that increase economic capacity and productivity these people create income and wealth for thousands or even millions of employees and stakeholders. Everyone benefits. You want these people to get as rich as they can because they do it by building an enterprise that is valuable to the nation.

Making Capitalism Work Again

The Productive Capitalists are as concerned as everyone else about the growing wealth and income gap. Most would like to see the problem solved. Most need the problem to be solved because it is very difficult to build a vibrant growing company in an economy that isn't thriving and growing. Even Productive Capitalists end up running zero sum companies if the economy is not structured to utilize the productivity gains they create. They are the "Accidental Zero Sum Capitalists".

Society needs to devise more ways of supporting the "Productive Capitalists," particularly when there is a need for supply stimulation, and limiting the ability of the "Zero Sum Gain Capitalists" to game the system. A basis for doing this is that "Productive Capitalists" tend to make long-term investments and "Zero Sum Gain Capitalists" tend to hold their investments for a short time. There shouldn't be a tax on capital gains. Instead, there should be a tax on capital withdrawals. As long as the capital is invested in the productive capacity of the nation it benefits all citizens and it should not be taxed, but when capital is withdrawn for personal use or foreign investment taxes should apply.

41. Summary

"Trade for debt" has broken the *productivity coupling* that linked productivity and wages and that caused the middle class to prosper in the Golden Age of Capitalism between 1945 and 1970. This has caused the economy to become demand constrained.

In order to get the economy growing again and to make capitalism work for everyone, especially low income and middle income workers, the *productivity coupling* between worker's wages and productivity must be restored so that there is *income participation*.

Productivity is likely to increase over 30 percent in the next ten years. There will be significant substitution of capital for labor. If wages are coupled to productivity increases, then the standard of living for all workers will increase by over 30 percent. If there is no *productivity coupling* to wages the wealth of the middle and lower income classes will continue to decline. If there is no *income participation* then there must be *income redistribution* where high-income earners and capital are taxed and the proceeds redistributed to low-income earners, otherwise capitalism will entirely stop working for all but the rich.

The Federal Reserve must be given the power to effectively regulate the economy using the principles of the "*Productivity Equilibrium Model*" to maximize economic growth, ensure that workers participate in that growth, and balance supply and demand.

Making Capitalism Work Again

The increasing wealth gap between the rich and the rest cannot go on forever if over half of society is suffering a declining standard of living. Long-term social stability requires either wealth redistribution or economic participation for low and middle income groups.

Thomas Piketty's book *Capitalism in the Twenty First Century* can be condensed down to one equation. Piketty argues that the reason for the increasing income and wealth gap is that $r > g$ (the rate of return on capital is greater than growth).

This book can be reduced down to a few equations. The reason for the declining standard of living for low and middle income workers is that wage growth is less than productivity growth; ($wg < pg$), which causes consumption growth to be less than productivity growth; ($cg < pg$)

To solve the problem, wage growth must be greater than productivity growth. If $wg > pg$, then over the long term $cg > pg$ and corporations will grow and middle-class prosperity will also begin to grow again.

The next step is for economists, academics and politicians to debate whether it is possible to change the way the economy works so that $wg > pg$, as it was during the Golden Age of Capitalism.

42. Fundamental Truths

These fundamental truths are self-evident:

The US economy is demand constrained. Supply far exceeds demand. Supply and demand must be in balance for an economy to prosper and grow.

Productivity will continue to increase, possibly rapidly, due to Artificial Intelligence, automation and robotics. This will increase supply and reduce employment and wages, thus further reducing demand and causing low inflation or deflation.

The only viable way to increase demand is to increase consumer spending.

The only viable way to increase consumer spending is to increase the median income.

The only way to increase the median income given increasing productivity is for government to implement a *"basic income"* or to raise wages.

If voters choose Social Democracy and the *"basic income"* option, it will spell the end of liberal democracy. Milton Freidman talks about this in his book Capitalism and Freedom.

The *Productivity Equilibrium Model* with *income participation* is the best way to raise wages. ***The "Productivity Equilibrium Model" is the best Liberal Democracy (conservative) solution proposal on the table.***

Productivity Economics will align the interests of capital and labor. Both benefit when productivity increases as opposed to the status quo where it is win/lose when productivity increases.

The "Productivity Equilibrium Model" is the best way to make capitalism work for everybody.

43. Necessity and Sufficiency Test

Any policy proposal must pass the test of being both necessary and sufficient to solve the problem being addressed.

There have been many initiatives to get the US and the world economy growing again, including negative interest rates, expanded infrastructure spending, expanded or restricted international trade, extreme expansion of the money supply and the various tax regime changes proposed by different political candidates. None of these programs will work to solve the low growth, low demand problem or the income and wealth gap and declining middle class income problem, because they do not pass the test of being both *sufficient* and *necessary*.

Giving the Federal Reserve control of the national minimum wage to ensure that low-income workers share the benefits of productivity increases is *sufficient* to solve the low growth, low inflation/deflation, lack of demand, and declining middle-class standard of living problems.

A *balanced trade mandate* is *necessary* to allow the national minimum wage policy to work and to realize the trade gains from comparative advantage. Without it, production will move to lower-cost jurisdictions when the minimum wage is increased and the benefits will be lost.

A new corporate tax regime is *necessary* to efficiently implement the *balanced trade mandate*, and to remove tax distortions that make the international playing field uneven. Uneven tax regimes are effectively subsidies, and the USA is on the wrong end of those subsidies.

44.   A Steve Jobs Moment

We need a Steve Jobs moment. We need economic elegance.

We need to transform a system of international trade and finance from one that is inefficient and distorted, inherently unstable, incredibly complex requiring millions of lawyers, accountants and bureaucrats to operate, into a simple system of balanced trade, uniform tariffs, and simple taxes that promote stable economic growth, and increasing wealth for the middle class. It needs to be self-regulating and able to operate more or less autonomously outside the sphere of political influence.

The policies proposed in this book will turn the economy around. It will recreate the conditions of the Golden Age of Capitalism between 1945 and 1970. Demand will increase. Employment will increase and real incomes and standards of living will increase. Assets, including savings and capital, will begin to appreciate. Corporate revenues and profits will grow. Companies will invest in America.

A virtuous circle will be reborn. The Federal Reserve will once again have the problem of controlling inflation. The traditional tools will work and hopefully this time we will be wise enough and have the tools to prevent a new bubble forming. It will be the "Platinum Age of Capitalism."

Young people will have a future. They are the future, so if we don't act now there is no future.

45.　The Other Side of the Story

This book makes the case that trade imbalances are a transfer of wealth, and that if we want to improve the lot of the middle class in the USA trade imbalances must be eliminated.

Over the past 50 years Japan, Korea, and China, and many other emerging economies have all experienced strong economic expansions, all driven by surging exports and trade surpluses in the early phases of the expansion. As discussed earlier, to a large degree this has been a transfer of wealth from developed countries to emerging countries.

This book argues that this massive wealth transfer occurred at the expense of the middle class in the first world countries.

Another way to look at it is that it has been the most successful economic development program in the history of mankind. Over a billion people have been lifted out of poverty. The world median income has skyrocketed, and worldwide poverty has plummeted to the lowest levels in history. Increasing world trade has done more to eliminate poverty than all the aid and charity programs combined, and it is sustainable.

Yes, this was mostly done at the expense of the middle class in America and Europe, but perhaps it is for the greater good. The standard of living of the middle class in the West hasn't really fallen much, it has just been stagnant for a long time.

Mandated balanced trade may cut off this path to prosperity for other third world countries, but more likely the worldwide free trade that the policy creates will accelerate trade and wealth creation in third world countries that have good democratic government and liberal economic policies.

The fact of the matter is that everything this book advocates; balanced trade, productivity being fed back into the economy, real positive interest rates etc. is being done at a world scale. By definition trade is balanced at a "world level." Productivity is growing extremely rapidly in countries like China, India and Eastern Europe. When you move large portions of your society from the agricultural sector to the manufacturing sector there are massive gains in productivity. Those productivity gains are being coupled back into the world economy in the form of rapidly rising wages and standards of living in those countries. The benefits of productivity gains are being coupled to the world population, but in a haphazard way that increases systematic risk.

It is not rocket science. That path to prosperity is well worn. The benefits are being accrued at a world level, but partially at the expense of the Western world.

It is not necessary for the Western world to sacrifice its wellbeing for the emerging markets to prosper. Thriving economies in the West combined with open balanced trade will accelerate progress in the emerging markets. It is all about productivity growth. The productivity gains that come from innovation are not a zero sum game.

There is evidence that wages are beginning to grow slower than productivity improvements in China and emerging markets, possibly due to increasing levels of automation and growing capital utilization in those countries. If wages decouple from productivity in emerging economies declining middle class incomes will become a world problem rather than just a Western world problem and the world economy will be in serious trouble. [52]

China needs the *"Productivity Equilibrium Model"* approach as much as any country. China has reached the limits of export driven growth. They have become too big. China is struggling with how to transition from an export-led economy to a consumption-based economy. To continue growing and providing employment for its people China must adopt the Golden Age model of balanced trade, productivity growth maximization, and productivity coupled wage growth. The *"Productivity Equilibrium Model"* is the way forward for China.

46. The Future

No one can predict the future. Predictions of the future are always extrapolations of the past, based on what we think we know of the future discontinuities. However, we don't and can't know what the game changers will be. What are the discontinuities in the trend line caused by unknowable factors?

The big issues of today are global warming, the economy, terrorism, and the decline of the middle class.

The interesting thing is that, if you go back in increments of 30 years and determine what the big issues were then, almost none are issues after 30 years. Problems get solved. We are a creative, innovative society and necessity is the mother of invention.

The world is better today than it was when I was a child by almost every metric. The world keeps getting better because we innovate and change. Democracy and capitalism are systems that are proven to work over long periods of time to solve problems and make things better.

So providing we don't break democracy or capitalism, I predict that none of the big issues of today will be big issues in 30 years, because either a technological breakthrough will have solved the problem, or we will have changed the way we do things.

And I predict that the world standard of living will be universally higher in 30 years than it is today, unless we don't change the way we do things.

47.   About the Author

Ronald Hart is an engineer by profession.   He has a Bachelor of Applied Science degree from the University of British Columbia.   His career progression was engineer, basement inventor, entrepreneur and CEO of a two-hundred employee high tech company, and now author. He sold the company in 1999 and since then he has spent his time as an investor, angel investor, and adventure traveler sailing, skiing, hiking, scuba diving and touring around the world including one year sailing in the South Pacific with his wife on their sailboat. He has spent considerable time studying and trying to understand how the economy works. His reasoning is influenced by his knowledge of control theory; a branch of engineering and mathematics that deals with the behavior of dynamic systems involving feedback. Ron is Canadian and when they are not travelling or sailing he spends his time with his wife in their homes in Canada and Australia.

[1] European Life Insurers: Unsustainable Business Model. 5 May 2015. IMF Direct.
https://blog-imfdirect.imf.org/2015/05/05/european-life-insurers-unsustainable-business-model/

[2] Low Interest Rates. National Association of Insurance Commissioners. 18 Sept 2015.
http://www.naic.org/cipr_topics/topic_low_interest_rates.htm

[3] How Will the Fourth Industrial Revolution Affect Economic Policy. 28 Jan 2016. World Economic Forum.
http://www.weforum.org/agenda/2016/01/how-will-the-fourth-industrial-revolution-affect-economic-policy

[4] The compensation-productivity gap: a visual essay. Jan 2011 and 2015 update. Susan Fleck, John Glaser, and Shawn Sprague. Bureau of Labor Statistics. http://www.bls.gov/opub/mlr/2011/01/art3full.pdf

[5] Labor and Productivity Costs. 4 Feb 2016. Bureau of Labor Statistics.
http://www.bls.gov/lpc/prodybar.htm

[6] Federal Reserve Bank of St Louis series FEDMINNFRWG, **COMPRNFB**, OPHNFB and CPIAUCSL. Real hourly compensation is the hourly cost to businesses, adjusted for price changes, of wages, salaries, and benefits paid to workers.
Also see https://fredblog.stlouisfed.org/2015/07/the-real-minimum-wage/
and Understanding the Historic Divergence Between Productivity and a Typical Workers Pay. 2 Sept 2015. Economic Policy Institute.
http://www.epi.org/publication/understanding-the-historic-divergence-between-productivity-and-a-typical-workers-pay-why-it-matters-and-why-its-real/

[7] Bretton Wood System. Wikipedia
https://en.m.wikipedia.org/wiki/Bretton_Woods_system

[8] Lost Decade Japan. Wikipedia
https://en.wikipedia.org/wiki/Lost_Decade_(Japan)

9   Corporate Income Tax Rates. Organization For Economic Cooperation (OECD) Table II.1
http:/stats.oecd.org/index.aspx?DataSetCode=TABLE_II1

10   Big US Firms hold $2.1 Trillion Overseas to avoid taxes. 6 Oct 2015. Reuters
http://www.reuters.com/article/us-usa-tax-offshore-idUSKCN0S008U20151006

11   Companies of the United States with untaxed profits / Wikipedia
https://en.wikipedia.org/wiki/Companies_of_the_United_States_with_untaxed_profits

12 The Pfizer-Allergan merger is a huge tax dodge. 23 Nov 2015. Vox
http://www.vox.com/2015/11/23/9784956/pfizer-allergan-merger

Is the Pfizer-Allergan Deal Unpatriotic? 24 Nov 2015. The Atlantic.
http://www.theatlantic.com/business/archive/2015/11/pfizer-allergan-merger-tax-haven/417492/

13 Johnson Controls press release 25 Jan 2016.
http://www.johnsoncontrols.com/media-center/news/press-releases/2016/01/25/johnson-controls-and-tyco-to-merge

14 The Age of Diminishing Expectations. Paul Krugman
http://www.amazon.com/The-Diminished-Expectations-Third-Edition/dp/0262611341

15 Productivity /Wikipedia https://en.wikipedia.org/wiki/Productivity

16 Gross Domestic Product / Wikipedia
https://en.wikipedia.org/wiki/Gross_domestic_product

17 Don't Expect Consumer Spending to be the Engine of Economic Growth It Once Was. William Emmons. Jan 2012. St Louis Fed article
https://www.stlouisfed.org/Publications/Regional-Economist/January-2012/Dont-Expect-Consumer-Spending-To-Be-the-Engine-of-Economic-Growth-It-Once-Was

18 Prisoners' Dilemma explanation. Library of Economics and Liberty.
http://www.econlib.org/library/Enc/PrisonersDilemma.html

[19] Why are Corporations Hoarding Trillions? Adam Davidson, 20 Jan 2016. New York Times.
http://www.nytimes.com/2016/01/24/magazine/why-are-corporations-hoarding-trillions.html

[20] Historical Series; US International Trade in Good and Services. United States Census Bureau.
http://www.census.gov/foreign-trade/statistics/historical/index.html

[21] Measures of Central Tendency For Wage Data. USA Social Security Administration.
https://www.ssa.gov/oact/cola/central.html

[22] Daily Yield Curve Rates. US Department of the Treasury.
https://www.treasury.gov/resource-center/data-chart-center/interest-rates/Pages/TextView.aspx?data=yieldYear&year=2015

[23] Total Business Sales. Federal Reserve Bank of St Louis.
Series TOTBUSSMSA
https:/research.stlouisfed.org/fred2

[24] OECD Statistical Profile of the European Union, 2013
http://www.oecd-ilibrary.org/economics/country-statistical-profile-european-union_20752288-table-eu

[25] Reform the International monetary system essay By Zhou Xiaochaun, People's Bank of China. 23 Mar 2009.
www.bis.org/review/r090402c.pdf

[26] Global Rebalancing and the Bancor. John Aziz. 22 July 2013. Pieria
http://www.pieria.co.uk/articles/global_rebalancing__the_bancor

[27] Characteristics of Minimum Wage Workers 2014, Apr 2015, Report 1054, Bureau of Labor Statistics report.
http://www.bls.gov/opub/reports/cps/characteristics-of-minimum-wage-workers-2014.pdf

[28] US Department of Agriculture; Supplemental Nutrition Assistance Program reports
http://www.fns.usda.gov/pd/supplemental-nutrition-assistance-program-snap
http://www.fns.usda.gov/sites/default/files/pd/34SNAPmonthly.pdf

[29] The Cost of Redistributing Wealth, Noah Smith, 25 Nov 2015, Bloomberg View http://www.bloombergview.com/articles/2015-11-25/leaving-the-justice-out-of-wealth-redistribution

[30] MIT Living Wage Calculator. http://livingwage.mit.edu   Go to the bottom and select a location.
Wikipedia Living Wage: https://en.wikipedia.org/wiki/Living_wage

[31] World Bank Central Government Debt by Country data http://data.worldbank.org/indicator/GC.DOD.TOTL.GD.ZS/countries

[32] Characteristics of Minimum Wage Workers 2014 report 1054, April 2015. US Bureau of Labor Statistics. http://www.bls.gov/opub/reports/cps/characteristics-of-minimum-wage-workers-2014.pdf

[33] Characteristics of Minimum Wage Workers 2014 report 1054, April 2015. US Bureau of Labor Statistics. http://www.bls.gov/opub/reports/cps/characteristics-of-minimum-wage-workers-2014.pdf

[34] Employed Full time median weekly earnings. Federal Reserve Bank of St Louis. Series LEU0254658200A https://research.stlouisfed.org/fred2/series/LEU0254658200A

[35] Raise That Wage, Paul Krugman, Princeton University, 17 February 2013; The New York Times http://www.nytimes.com/2013/02/18/opinion/krugman-raise-that-wage.html?_r=1

[36] Raise the Minimum Wage article, Editorial Board, Bloomberg View, 18 April 2012 http://www.bloombergview.com/articles/2012-04-16/u-s-minimum-wage-lower-than-in-lbj-era-needs-a-raise

[37] OECD Minimum Wages by Country Table. http://stats.oecd.org/Index.aspx?DataSetCode=RMW

[38] Global Price Info: Big Max Index.
http://www.globalprice.info/en/?p=statistics/bigmac&sort=bigmac1

[39] The Great Disruption: From Brawn to Brain (excerpt), Dr. Ed Yardini Blog; 29 Dec 2015.
http://blog.yardeni.com/2015_12_01_archive.html

[40] The Fourth Industrial Revolution: what it mans and how to respond, Klaus Schwab, 14 Jan 2016, World Economic forum, Davos.
http://www.weforum.org/agenda/2016/01/the-fourth-industrial-revolution-what-it-means-and-how-to-respond

[41] Social Democracy / Wikipedia
https://en.m.wikipedia.org/wiki/Social_democracy

[42] Finland considers basic income to reform welfare system, Maija Unkuri, 20 Aug 2015, BBC News
http://www.bbc.com/news/world-europe-33977636

[43] Presidential candidate Bernie Sanders "absolutely sympathetic" to basic income approach, Karl Widerquist, Basic Income News, 28 July 2015.
http://www.basicincome.org/news/2015/07/bernie-sanders-absolutely-sympathetic-basic-income/

[44] Liberalism / Wikipedia
https://en.m.wikipedia.org/wiki/Liberalism

[45] 2007 Schools Wikipedia Selection. McGill University. The Liberalism Series
http://www.cs.mcgill.ca/~rwest/wikispeedia/wpcd/wp/l/Liberalism.htm

[46] What is a Republican? Republican Definition/ Core Beliefs. 11 April 2014, Republicanviews org.
http://www.republicanviews.org/what-is-a-republican-republican-definition/

[47] It's Still Not the End of History, Timothy Stanley and Alexander Lee, 1 Sept 2014, The Atlantic

152

http://www.theatlantic.com/politics/archive/2014/09/its-still-not-the-end-of-history-francis-fukuyama/379394/

[48] How the Economy Helps Trump, Zachary Karabell, 10 Dec 2015, Politico Magazine
http://www.politico.com/magazine/story/2015/12/donald-trump-2016-economy-213428

[49] Wal-Mart Plans to Give Raises to 1.1 Million US Workers, Shannon Pettypiece, 21Jan 2016, Bloomberg Business
http://www.bloomberg.com/news/articles/2016-01-20/wal-mart-to-give-raise-to-1-1-million-u-s-workers-next-month

[50] High Expectations, What a big pay rise at Walmart means for the minimum wage debate, 30 Jan 2016, The Economist
http://www.economist.com/news/united-states/21689607-what-big-pay-rise-walmart-means-minimum-wage-debate-high-expectations

[51]Zero Sum Game Definition, Investopedia
http://www.investopedia.com/terms/z/zero-sumgame.asp

[52] Global Wage Report 2014/15, Wages and Income inequality, International Labor Organization
http://www.ilo.org/wcmsp5/groups/public/---dgreports/---dcomm/---publ/documents/publication/wcms_324678.pdf

www.ingramcontent.com/pod-product-compliance
Lightning Source LLC
Chambersburg PA
CBHW070320190526
45169CB00005B/1680